IN MY
FATHER'S HOUSE

Corrie ten Boom

with C.C. Carlson

IN MY FATHER'S HOUSE

The years before "The Hiding Place"

Guideposts

Carmel, New York 10512

Library of Congress Cataloging in Publication Data

Ten Boom, Corrie.
    In my father's house.

    1. Ten Boom, Corrie.   I.   Carlson, Carole C., joint author.   II.   Title.
    BR1725.T35A34   269'.2'0924 [B]   75-45373
    ISBN 0-8007-0783-4

When my parents were married, many years ago, they claimed Psalms 32:8 as their "life verse," the promise which they felt was God's assurance for them.

I will instruct thee and teach thee in the way which thou shalt go: I will guide thee with mine eye.

. . . this promise became the special directive for my life as well.

CORRIE TEN BOOM
From *Tramp for the Lord*

Contents

Foreword

Today I know that memories are the key not to the past, but to the future. I know that the experiences of our lives, when we let God use them, become the mysterious and perfect preparation for the work He will give us to do.

Corrie wrote that in *The Hiding Place,* without realizing that it had provided the introduction to this book.

As I worked with Corrie, following her around America, and living with her in Holland, I saw her in many different circumstances. It is a constant amazement to me how the Lord uses her. One time my husband, Ward, and I prayed with her in a small room off a large auditorium. She was ashen with pain and weariness. When she walked on the stage before four thousand people, her voice was firm and her message animated. She was—and continues to be—a living example of the way in which the Spirit of the Lord works through His available servant.

However, as *In My Father's House* began to grow, I became excited to see how this was more than a collection of memories —more than nostalgia from a rich life. Here we had the unique lessons of a family preparing for a future, a future which would demand the power of God's love and strength.

If we are living in the time in which we believe God's plan for planet earth is reaching its completion—when the new beginning Jesus promised would take place—then each individual and family needs the pattern for living in this present age. Never before in human history have guidelines been more important.

The applications of various parts of Corrie's life to modern living were impressed upon me, as I savored those wonderful "years before." I've learned so much for my own life and family, as I've lived with Corrie *In My Father's House*. Let's visit together . . . .

CAROLE C. CARLSON

IN MY
FATHER'S HOUSE

1

Inheritance

"Remarkable, extraordinary . . . Peter, where did Cook find strawberries in the midst of winter?"

The Dutch merchant summoned his butler and pointed to the luscious fruit in the silver compote. Even in the home of great wealth this was an amazing luxury in the early 1800s.

"It's the gardener, sir . . . ten Boom. He does some miraculous things in that hothouse of his."

"Ten Boom, you say. Hmm, must remember him. Astounding! Bring me some more, Peter, with lots of thick cream."

My great-grandfather ten Boom grew those plump strawberries during the chilling months when ruddy-cheeked children skated over the canals. He was no ordinary gardener, but a master craftsman who caressed the soil into performing miracles. He experimented with plants, manipulating them between an ice cellar and a hothouse, until he produced the fruit which was served at the dinner table of his employer, one of the richest men in Hofstede, Bronstede, Heemstede.

Those simple strawberries saved my great-grandfather from jail!

It was during the time of Napoleon; Europe was trembling from the onslaught of the evil little man from Corsica. Swaggering across the continent, victorious in war, the French emperor conquered country after country, and forced men into submission. The government of Holland was ruled by Napoleon's followers and their oppressive regime.

My great-grandfather was an independent man; he had spunk, but not much tact, I'm afraid. He refused to submit to men who denied freedom to other men. However, Hollanders at that time had two alternatives: they were either obedient to those who served the strutting dictator; or they faced what could be very severe punishment.

Tyranny at any time in man's history demands loyalty.

One Sunday Great-grandfather went to his church and heard the minister announce the opening hymn; the theme was from Psalms 21, but as the congregation began to understand the words, one voice after another stopped. They realized it was a pointed description of their political situation. Nobody dared to continue.

But Great-grandfather and the minister sang louder, a defiant duet (translated from the Dutch):

> The evil one considers himself to be free from all bondage, and runs around, while he stirs the people. At the same time, the bad people assume they hold the reins of government, and they are being raised to the summits of honor.

Sad hearts and silent voices were encouraged by the bravery of the minister and the spunky gardener.

When news of ten Boom's traitorous act of defiance reached the authorities, he received a summons to appear at the town hall. He must have been prepared for the consequences, as he addressed the officer in charge.

"What does this Mr. Snotneus [snot-nose] want with me?"

First he challenged the regime; then he hurled that contemptuous name at his accuser!

But where do strawberries fit into all this? Before Great-grandfather had a chance to be sentenced or taken to prison, his boss, who was a very influential citizen, interceded and had him pardoned. (A gardener couldn't grow fruit in jail, could he?)

My father told us this story of Great-grandfather and his personal challenge to the Napoleonic regime with a sense of joy.

"I'm glad he was a real man," Father said.

Over a hundred years later when people said to Father, "Stop having Jews in your house—you will be sent to prison," my father answered, "I am too old for prison life, but if that should happen, then it would be, for me, an honor to give my life for God's ancient people, the Jews."

From Generation to Generation

Willem ten Boom, my grandfather, was not strong like his father, so he chose a work which was not physically difficult. In the year 1837, Grandfather purchased a little house in Haarlem for four hundred guilders, and set up shop as a watchmaker.

It was in 1844 that Grandfather had a visit from his minister, Dominee Witteveen, who had a special request. "Willem, you know the Scriptures tell us to pray for the peace of Jerusalem and the blessing of the Jews."

"Ah, yes, Dominee, I have always loved God's ancient people —they gave us our Bible and our Savior."

Beginning with this conversation, a prayer fellowship was started, with Grandfather and his friends praying for the Jewish people. This was an unusual idea among Christians at that time. The Jews were scattered throughout the world, without a country or a national identity; Jerusalem was a city torn by centuries of conflict. The attention of the world was not upon the Middle East, and yet a small group of Dutch believers met in a little Haarlem house, a watchmaker's shop (later called the Beje), to read the Scriptures and pray for the Jews.

In a divine way which is beyond our human understanding, God answered those prayers. It was in the same house, exactly one hundred years later, that Grandfather's son, my father, and four of his grandchildren, and one great-grandson were arrested for helping save the lives of Jews during the German occupation of Holland.

Another strutting dictator, more arrogant and insane than Napoleon, had planned to exterminate every Jew in the world. When Holland was controlled by Hitler's troops, many Jews were killed.

For helping and hiding the Jews, my father, my brother's son, and my sister all died in prison. My brother survived his imprisonment, but died soon afterward. Only Nollie, my older sister, and I came out alive.

So many times we wonder why God has certain things happen to us. We try to understand the circumstances of our lives, and we are left wondering. But God's foolishness is so much wiser than our wisdom.

From generation to generation, from small beginnings and little lessons, He has a purpose for those who know and trust Him.

God has no problems—just plans!

Beginning With Mama

My mother was a woman with a loving sense of humor and a striking appearance. She had thick, dark, curly hair, and brilliant blue eyes—an unusual combination for a Hollander. She came from a large family, and was left fatherless just after her mother gave birth to an eighth baby. While she was still very young, her mother and her brothers and sisters were forced to earn their own living.

One of her sisters, Jans, started a kindergarten where Cor (my mother) and another sister, Anna, became her assistants. I'm sure this experience helped my mother later in training her own children.

When Jans added a Sunday school to her kindergarten, she began to work with a young theology student, Hendrik Wildeboer, who became her special boyfriend. Cor caught the eye of a handsome teacher in the Sunday school by the name of Casper ten Boom, and they immediately found something in common: their birthdays were on the same day, May 18.

Romance grew between Cor and Casper; when Cor journeyed to Harderwijk to visit her grandmother, Casper was so lonely that he followed her the next day.

About fifty years later, I visited the quaint village of Harderwijk on the Zuider Zee with Father. As we walked along the Bruggestraat, Father said, "This is where I proposed to your mother. There were cobblestones instead of pavement at that time, but many of the old houses and the sea gate are still the same."

He paused to remember the youth which had vanished, and his love for the gentle woman with the laughing eyes.

"Did Mother say *yes* immediately?" I asked.

"No, not until the next day, and I spent a very restless night waiting for that decision!"

When I asked him if he had ever regretted his decision to marry Mama, his voice was firm. "Never! Until the last day of her life, I was just as much in love with your mother as I was on that day in Harderwijk. We didn't have an easy life—we had many sorrows—but God led us by His extraordinary providence."

A Little Jewelry Store

Grandmother died shortly before Casper and Cor were married. By then, Father had started a jewelry store in a small house in the heart of the Jewish section of Amsterdam.

Once a customer arrived who was a pastor from Ladysmith, South Africa. He came into the shop and asked Father to provide a clock and a bell for his church tower. This was a tremendous encouragement to a young merchant. The order was simple to fill; all Father had to do was to go to the factory in Brabant to make the selection; the manufacturer did all the installation. However, the commission from that sale provided enough money for the young Dutch couple to be married.

Uncle Hendrik, Jans's husband, was a minister in a little village near Amsterdam. Mother and Father had to go to the town hall first, to be registered and married in a civil ceremony. The man at the town hall who married them thought they were "high people" because they came from Amsterdam. He tried to be very dignified, in a manner suitable for this distinguished couple, and began the marriage speech with great airs.

"Honored bride and bridegroom . . . you are now . . . you are now gathered . . . you are now gathered here . . . ." He stopped, looked around, and burst into tears.

Father said, "I'm so touched by your speech and tears, but we would like to be married."

The poor fellow finished the ceremony somehow, but Uncle Hendrik conducted the final marriage rites in his church—without tears.

The newlyweds moved into a shabby little house in Amsterdam after their wedding. It's probably just as well that the emotional clerk from the town hall didn't know of their humble means!

Mother had dreamed of a home with a small garden, for she loved flowers and the beauty of color.

"I love to see much of the sky," she often said.

The sky was there, if she stretched far enough to see it in the narrow street outside the old house. Their cramped home had a single room on each story, with worn-out furniture left by my grandmother.

Money was scarce, but happiness was abundant.

The neighborhood of Jewish people made it possible for Father to participate in their Sabbaths and other holy days. He studied the Old Testament, their Talmud, with them, and was given opportunities to understand and explain the fulfillment of the prophecies of the Old Testament in the New Testament.

My father's love for the Jewish people was nurtured in the Jewish quarter of Amsterdam during those first years of married life. Father and Mother lived on poverty's edge, and yet their contentment was not dependent upon their surroundings. Their relationship with each other and with the Lord gave them strength.

Plan for Parenthood

When the first baby was expected Mother was glad she had learned to sew. She had inherited an old sewing machine from

Mother with Willem and Betsie.

her mother, and every moment she could find she stitched little garments for the baby. A Jewess who lived upstairs couldn't contain her curiosity, and asked Mother if she was a seamstress.

"No," Mother answered proudly, "but I'm expecting my first baby. See the little dress I've made?" She held up a dainty garment tenderly.

The Jewess was astonished. "You're not sewing the clothes before the baby arrives! That is tempting God!"

Mother was puzzled, but this didn't stop her from preparing for her baby. However, she began to understand why Mary had only swaddling clothes for the Baby Jesus. It wasn't lack of money, but the Jewish custom not to sew the layette before the birth of the child. I've heard that Portuguese Jews maintain this tradition today.

When Betsie, the first child, was born, Mother became quite ill. She asked her youngest sister, Anna, to come for a few weeks to help with the new baby. Those few weeks stretched into forty years.

Mother and Anna had always been close, but when Mother married, Anna went to live with Jans and Uncle Hendrik. Anna, however, became very lonely for Cor, and was delighted when Mother and Father invited her to stay with them in Amsterdam.

Within seven years, four more babies were born, but one didn't live. Father had to look for a cheaper house to accommodate his growing responsibilities.

By the time I was born, they were living on the Korte Prinsegracht, in a house at the very end of the canal, where few people passed the shop. Business was at its lowest ebb.

I was a premature baby, with blue skin and pinched features. When Uncle Hendrik saw me he shook his head sadly. "I hope the Lord will quickly take this poor little creature to His home in heaven," he said.

Fortunately, my parents didn't feel the same as Uncle Hendrik. They surrounded me with love and good care. There were no incubators in those days, and one of the greatest problems was keeping me warm. I cried so pitifully from the cold that

Tante Anna rolled me in her apron, and tied me against her body; then I became warm and quiet.

Many years later while I was in Africa I met a missionary family whose baby could not be comforted, until a native girl bound the child to her back with a piece of cloth. The baby became calm, secure in the closeness to the body of a person who loved him.

I must have felt that same way bound snugly in Tante Anna's apron.

Throughout the first year of my life I was a poor, sickly-looking creature. Mother told me that once she was traveling by train with a friend who held a beautiful, plump baby on her lap. The baby's name was Rika, and the people in the coach were giving her many admiring glances and comments. They would look at me in my mother's arms, and then turn away, unable to find anything positive to say.

Mother told me this bothered her at first, but then she would hug me and whisper, "I wouldn't exchange you for anyone in the whole world, you darling ugly baby with the beautiful eyes."

When Rika was two years old, she began having epileptic seizures. I played with her all through my childhood, but I remember how aware I was that her little face would change so drastically as the sickness would overpower her. Mother was always ready to care for Rika; throughout her life Mother taught us to be helpful and loving toward those who were weak or abnormal.

Haarlem Inheritance

Grandfather Willem died when I was six months old, leaving Father his shop in Haarlem. We moved into the house, which wasn't very large, and poor Mother still didn't have her garden. She put some flower pots on the flat roof and called this her yard. She had geraniums in clay pots, hanging fuchsia, and some ivy climbing the brick wall. She developed a roof garden long before the modern penthouse dwellers thought of such a thing.

Even in the "new" house in Haarlem, she could see only a small piece of the sky she loved. The roof became her "outdoors" when she became too weak to take her daily walks in the street.

During those first years of their marriage, the financial situation must have been very serious. Anna worked night and day to nurse Mother when she was ill, and to care for four children. She earned the grand sum of one guilder (about thirty cents) a week. Father gave her this magnificent salary each Saturday, but often by the following Wednesday the finances would become so desperate that Father would have to go to the kitchen and ask, "Anna, do you still have your guilder?"

Anna always had the guilder available, and it often bought the food for the family on that day. This was certainly "blessed money."

This was the beginning of my rich inheritance. When I remember my family life, I realize that my parents and my aunts had truly mastered the art of living. They enjoyed life and they loved children.

"We never laughed so much as when you children were small," Tante Anna often said.

In our hearts we must have stored some of the memory of laughter to be brought out in later years, when the sounds of happy voices were scarce in our beloved land.

2

Five Is Not Too Young

In 1892, the year I was born, Holland was entering an exciting and important era. In a few years, Wilhelmina would be crowned Queen at the tender age of eighteen. There were signs which indicated that the stability of that latter part of the nineteenth century would soon be rocked by the rattling of German swords. Foreign policy was being shaped around lines of power, as young Kaiser Wilhelm II ruled the country which later played such an important part in my life.

History in the making means nothing to a child, but it was a world event for me when Mother or Tante Anna pinched a guilder hard enough to squeeze out some sugar and butter for those fat little sugar cookies I loved. The fragrance of baking would float from the iron stove into the shop, and tantalize the customers just as it put us in a happy mood.

When I was five years old, I learned to read; I loved stories, particularly those about Jesus. He was a member of the ten Boom family—it was just as easy to talk to Him as it was to carry on a conversation with my mother and father, my aunts, or my brother and sisters. He was there.

One day my mother was watching me play house. In my little girl world of fantasy, she saw that I was pretending to call on

Betsie, Willem, Nollie, and Corrie.

a neighbor. I knocked on the make-believe door and waited . . .
no one answered.

"Corrie, I know Someone who is standing at your door and
knocking right now."

Was she playing a game with me? I know now that there
was a preparation within my childish heart for that moment;
the Holy Spirit makes us ready for acceptance of Jesus Christ,
of turning our life over to Him.

"Jesus said that He is standing at the door, and if you invite
Him in He will come into your heart," my mother continued.
"Would you like to invite Jesus in?"

At that moment my mother was the most beautiful person
in the whole world to me.

"Yes, Mama, I want Jesus in my heart."

So she took my little hand in hers and we prayed together.
It was so simple, and yet Jesus Christ says that we all must
come as children, no matter what our age, social standing, or
intellectual background.

When Mother told me later about this experience, I recalled it clearly.

But, You're So Little

Does a child of five really know what he's doing? Some people say that children don't have spiritual understanding—that we should wait until a child can "make up his mind for himself." I believe a child should be led, not left to wander.

Jesus became more real to me from that time on. Mother told me later that I began to pray for others, as young as I was.

The street behind our house was the Smedestraat. It was filled with saloons, and many of the happenings there were frightening to me. As I played outside jumping rope, or joined with Nollie, my sister, in a game of *bikkelen* (ball and stones), I saw the police pick up these lurching, incoherent men as they slumped to the ground or slouched in a doorway, and take them into the police station.

I would stand before the *politie bureau* (police station) behind the Beje, and watch the drunks being pushed in. It made me shiver. The building was made of dark red brick, and 'way at the top were turrets with small windows. Were those the cells, I wondered?

It was in that same police station years later that my father, and all his children, and a grandson were taken after being arrested for helping Jews escape from the German gestapo.

As a child I would be so concerned for those arrested that I would run into the house sobbing, "Mother . . . I'm afraid those poor men are going to be hurt . . . they're so sick!"

Bless Mother's understanding. She would say, "Pray for them, Corrie."

And I would pray for the drunks. "Dear Jesus, please help those men . . . and Jesus, help all the people on the Smedestraat."

Many years later I spoke on a television station in Holland. I received a letter after the program which said: "My husband was especially interested because you told us that you had lived in Haarlem. He lived in a house on the Smedestraat. Three years ago he accepted the Lord Jesus as his Savior."

I read that letter and recalled the prayers of little Corrie. That man whose wife wrote me was one person I had prayed for seventy-six years before.

Does He Listen?

At another time in my later years I was camping with a number of Haarlem girls. Around the campfire one evening, we were talking about the Lord and chatting about the pleasant events of the day.

"Do you know that I am a neighbor of yours?" one of the girls asked me. "I live in the Smedestraat."

"I lived there until five years ago," said another girl.

"My mother lived there," said a third.

We all began to laugh to discover that all eighteen of those girls, who were sleeping in the big camp tent, had lived on that street or their parents had lived there. They found it an amusing coincidence.

"Listen," I said, "I just remembered something that I had almost forgotten. When I was five or six years old, I used to pray every day for the people in the Smedestraat. The fact that we have been talking about Jesus, and that God has even used me to reach some of your parents, is an answer to the prayer of a little child. Never doubt whether God hears our prayers, even the unusual ones."

How often we think when a prayer is not answered that God has said *no*. Many times He has simply said, *"Wait."*

The Future Comes Quickly

When we are very young the future is so hard to grasp. My father had one coming event which he mentioned in every prayer. It baffled me. I didn't want to ask in front of the entire family; I thought they might think I was foolish to ask about something I heard several times a day.

I waited until Father came upstairs to tuck me in; this was a time I could ask him anything.

"Papa, you always pray in every prayer, 'Let soon come that

great day when Jesus Christ, Your beloved Son, comes on the clouds of heaven.' Why are you longing for that day?"

"Correman, remember when you saw the men drunk and fighting in the Smedestraat, and they were taken to the police station? The whole world is filled with fighting. You may see worse fighting in your lifetime than what you have seen on the street."

I hoped not. Fighting upset me.

"In the Bible," Papa continued, "we read that Jesus has promised to come to this world to make everything new. The world is now covered with hatred, but when Jesus returns the world will be covered with the knowledge of God, like the water covers the bottom of the sea."

Thinking of that wonderful day, I knew why Papa prayed for it so often. "Oh, Papa, then everyone will know about Jesus! I'll be very happy when He comes."

Let the Children Come

Decades later I was speaking to a group when I challenged parents to "Bring your little ones to the Lord Jesus. He has said, 'Let the children come to me; the kingdom of God is theirs.'" (*See* Matthew 19:14.)

Then I told how I had made a decision for Jesus when I was five years old.

After that talk I left the platform, and went into a small room in the building where I found a father with two little boys, all on their knees. The father had an arm around both of those boys, and I moved back quietly while the man told the boys tenderly that they were not too young to ask Jesus to come into their hearts.

What a wonderful heritage those boys have, to know that their father cared enough about them to lead them to a knowledge of their heavenly Father!

Later I received a letter from a lady who told me the results in her life of that evening.

I went home after that meeting and went directly to my little girl, Mary, who was in bed. She knew about the

Mary, the little girl who died the day after she had accepted the Lord.

Lord because she had been to a Sunday school, but that night, in her bed, she gave her heart to Jesus.

The next morning she said, "Oh, Mommy, I'm so happy that Jesus is now in my heart. He made me a child of God."

Mary was singing the whole time before she went to school, and I was amazed that she sang many songs about heaven.

My husband went to school to pick her up that day, and as he approached the schoolhouse, he noticed that a great many people were standing around, and there obviously

28

must have been an accident. Then he saw what had happened.

Mary was on the street, her little body crumpled like a rag doll. She was dead.

As I read that letter my eyes were so filled with tears that the words blurred.

Mary had passed behind a big transport truck and had not seen another car, which was coming toward her from the other direction. She was killed immediately.

My husband brought her little body home. He was in deep despair, but then he remembered the songs Mary had sung that morning. I told him what had happened the evening before, and right then, my husband, who had never made a decision for the Lord Jesus, accepted Him as his Savior.

On Mary's burial day many children of her class came to the Lord.

I sat for a long time with that letter on my lap, realizing that I must have a new sense of urgency to talk to parents about the joy of leading their children to the Lord. What a wonderful assurance Mary's parents had to know that someday they would be with her again.

During some of my talks I have often repeated this little poem:

SAFE?

Said a precious little laddie,
To his father one bright day,
"May I give myself to Jesus,
Let Him wash my sins away?"

O, my son, but you're so little,
Wait until you older grow,
Bigger folks 'tis true, do need Him,
But little folk are safe, you know.

Said the father to his laddie,
As a storm was coming on,
"Are the sheep all safely sheltered,
Safe within the fold, my son?"

"All the big ones are, my father,
But the lambs, I let them go,
For I didn't think it mattered,
Little ones are safe, you know."

AUTHOR UNKNOWN

Praying for Crazy Thys

As a child in Haarlem I prayed for a man most people avoided. His nickname was *Gekke Thys* (Crazy Thys) and he was the town tramp, an idiot. I pitied him and when I was five or six years old started to talk about this to the Lord.

How curious the little minds of children are. Was it my mother or one of my aunts who gave me the advice to cast my burden on the Lord in prayer? Or did the Lord Himself give me this motivation?

Every prayer in the evening and in the morning ended with this request: "And Lord, be with all the people in the Smede-straat and also *Gekke Thys.*"

My sister, Nollie, was only a year and a half older than I, but she seemed so much wiser. I remember walking with her through the Smedestraat one day and stopping to watch a crowd of children surrounding someone they were taunting and teas-ing. As we inched closer to the others, wanting to know what was happening, but a bit afraid of getting involved in something which looked so mean, we realized that poor old Crazy Thys was standing in the middle of the circle, confusion and hurt showing in his face.

I was so full of pity for poor Thys and angry at the cruel children that I shouted, "You leave him alone, do you hear!"

The children stopped at my bold challenge. Thys looked for his defender and saw a little girl, less than half his size. Suddenly he walked toward me and stooped down. I could smell the

1895, Corrie and Nollie.

unpleasant odor of his unwashed clothes and matted beard. He put his hand under my chin and kissed me on both cheeks.

Nollie was shocked! She grabbed my hand and pulled me home as fast as we could run. Down the Smedestraat, into the alley which ran beside our house, and through the side door we raced.

"Aunty, someone . . . hurry! That dirty old *Gekke Thys* kissed Corrie. Let's wash her cheeks!"

My face was so thoroughly washed I was afraid my skin would fall off. I heard someone say, "Such dangerous tramps shouldn't be allowed to go so freely in the streets."

Stinging from the rebuke as well as the face scrubbing, I went to my mother. "Mama, why was it so bad that *Gekke Thys* kissed me? He's such a poor unhappy man. Everybody makes fun of him."

Mother took me into her bed and talked quietly with me as I nestled against her soft shoulder. She said, "Correman, it's good that you have pity for this man. The Lord Jesus gives you love for *Gekke Thys* and for the drunken men in the Smedestraat. Jesus loves sinners, but before they are going to love Him, these men can be very bad. It's wise to keep a little distance. But there's one great thing you and I can do—and you are doing that already—pray faithfully for them."

Shortly after that incident *Gekke Thys* disappeared from the streets. I don't know how the Lord worked in his life, but a deep concern for the feebleminded was fostered in me.

Fear No Evil . . . Except

A child is not fearless, contrary to what his parents may think at times. A child is often a bundle of unexpressed fears, unknown terrors, and shadowy worries. I was afraid of the doctor's office, my family's leaving me, and the mystery of death.

Nollie's nightgown was my contact with security. We slept in the same bed, and I can remember clinging to Nollie's nightgown as long as she would allow me. Poor Nollie, when she would try to turn, she would be anchored by my little fist clasping her tightly.

One time Mother took Nollie and me to visit a woman whose baby had died. I wished Nollie had been allowed to wear her nightgown on that journey, because I needed desperately to hang onto it.

We climbed a narrow staircase and entered the poorly furnished room of one of Mama's "lame ducks" (the name we children had given to her protégées). Although we often did not have sufficient money for ourselves, Mother always found someone who was in greater need.

In that shabby little room was a crib with a baby inside. It didn't move at all and its skin was very white. Nollie stood next to the crib and touched the baby's cheek.

"Feel that," she said to me, "it's so cold."

I touched the little hand, and then ran to my mother and buried my face in her lap. I had touched death for the first time, and it seemed that the impression of cold remained with me for hours and hours.

When we returned home, I ran up the narrow stairs to my bedroom and leaned against the antique chest of drawers. There was an enormous fear in my heart—almost terror. In my imagination, I pictured the future in which I saw myself all alone, my family gone, and myself left desolate. My family was my security, but that day I saw death, and knew that they could die, too. I had never thought about it before.

The dinner bell rang downstairs, and I was so grateful to go to the big oval table, and get warm again, and feel the security of being with my family. I thought how stupid the grown-ups would think I was if I told them about the fear which was still in my heart.

I ate dinner quietly that night, which was not easy when you are in the midst of such a lively family. Our dinner table spilled over with conversation.

After dinner Father took the Bible, as he always did, and began to read the lines from Psalms 46:2. "Therefore will not we fear, though the earth be removed, and though the mountains be carried into the midst of the sea" (KJV).

I sat up straight in my chair and stared at my father. I didn't know much about mountains, living in flat, flat Holland, but I certainly knew a lot about fear. I thought Papa must have known exactly what my problem was that night.

My faith in Papa, and in the words he read from the Bible, was absolute. If they said not to fear, then God would take care of it. I felt secure again.

3

From Small Beginnings

My doll, Casperina, and I were going to have a party! Mama and Tante Anna were cooking, and I watched their long skirts bustle past me from my perch on the footstool beneath the table. This was a wonderful place to play, safe and secure beneath the red and black tablecloth.

My friend was named after my father, but the resemblance ended there. I loved her very much, but dragging her up and down the stairs of the Beje had left her with a few fingers missing, and a slightly cracked head. Oh, my, why couldn't she look like Nollie's doll, who was immaculately dressed, and didn't have a scratch on her china face? Poor Casperina, she would never be in the same society with Emma, Betsie's doll, who was named after the mother of the Queen.

"Never mind, Casperina," I whispered to her in the shelter of our little house beneath the table, "Jesus loves you, and so do I."

When I was especially happy, I would sing a little song which Tante Jans had composed:

> *'k Zou zoo graag eens komen, Heiland,*
> *In dat heerlijk Vaderhuis.*

(I should just like to come, Savior,
In the beautiful Father-house.)

However, instead of singing *to come* I substituted *to peek*, combining my words with a mischievous look around the fat table leg.

Tante Anna laughed at me. "Corrie, you'd better not let Tante Jans hear you change the words in her songs. When she writes 'I should like to come to heaven,' that's what she means."

Some things grown-ups don't understand, I thought. I meant that it would be great fun just to look around for a moment in heaven, where I knew I would spend my future. I just wanted a little peek; after all my father-house right here on the Barteljorisstraat was all the heaven I wanted right then.

I clutched Casperina's three-fingered hand in mine and whispered, "We'll just stay in our own secret place, where no one will ever—ever—scold us for anything."

A Time to Uproot

A time comes when all children, even a little Dutch girl with her jaw set and her black-stockinged legs rigid upon the staircase, must leave her father's house for a time. I was born with my feet slightly turned in, a defect which the doctor said would cure itself with time and growth.

"Don't worry," he told Mama and Papa, "when she is about sixteen, she will become vain enough to turn her toes the right way."

However, when I turned my toes in even more, and tightened my fingers in a knuckle-whitening grip on the railing, I meant business.

"I'm not going to school. I know how to read; I can learn arithmetic from Papa, and Casperina needs me at home."

There. *That* was settled.

"Of course you're not going to school alone, Corrie. I am going to walk with you."

Papa bent over me, his beard tickling the top of my head, and one by one loosened my fingers on the railing. With the re-

lease of each finger, I howled a bit louder. By the time Papa
had my hand in his, he was almost dragging me down the street
toward school. I thought my hand would break—just like Casperina's—and then it would be impossible for me to go to school.

It must have taken great dignity for Papa, with his immaculate suit and erect carriage, to struggle past the homes and shops
of his friends with a red-faced child announcing her objections
to the entire world.

I knew Father was not angry, but his will was law. I had to
obey.

When we arrived at the school I saw a little boy being carried
into Master Robyns's classroom in his father's arms. (At least
I was walking!) He was crying lustily, even louder than I was.
He looked so ugly that I felt sorry for him. But what about me?
I realized how I must look to others, and stopped abruptly.

Papa released my hand; my fingers weren't broken at all—
only my heart was slightly injured. However, when Papa kissed
me gently on the cheek, bringing the familiar fragrance of
cigars and cologne, he assured me that when school was over,
he would be waiting at home, and I knew I would find that
blessed security I needed in the shelter of his arms.

God was teaching a little lesson in a small life, because sixty-
seven years later, He reminded me of my fingers on the railing.

I was in a room of *Zonneduin*, a house in Holland, which
some friends and I had established first for ex-prisoners who
had been in concentration camps, and later for any person who
needed nursing and rest. I had been traveling so much and was
tired—tired of strange beds and different food—tired of dressing
for breakfast—tired of new people, and new experiences. I liked
this very luxurious house with its large rooms, and decided
to stay, and enjoy the comfortable life in Holland, although
I knew that God didn't agree with my decision.

Most of the furniture in the entire house was mine, but there
was one room in particular which reminded me of the happy
family life of my past. It was a room which held my treasures:
photographs of those I loved, mementos of my family during
the years before. Every picture was like the railing on the stairs.

My hands grasped the past, and tried to hold on, but my heavenly Father's hands were stronger.

I left the house for a while for some speaking engagements, intending to return to my old room and settle in for good. However, when I came back to *Zonneduin* some weeks later, my pictures were down, and the strange belongings of someone else were on the bed.

My friends had not known of my personal decision to return to this room; my irregular life, my coming and going unexpectedly, was difficult for those who had to manage the big family of patients and staff in an orderly way.

But I decided to stay, and that was settled!

My heavenly Father spoke to me, "Only obey Me, Corrie. I'll hold your hand. It is My will that you leave your room. Later you will thank Me for this experience. You do not see it, but this is one of My great blessings for you."

Father's hand was firm, but I knew His love.

I packed up my suitcase again and left for the United States. How the Lord blessed my time there. Meetings began to grow in size, and when I saw people come from darkness into light, from bondage into liberation, I began to see the pattern. I could praise my Father that His hands were stronger than mine.

Blue Stones Can Hurt!

School life did not prove to be as horrible as I thought. I can still remember the sensation of victory when I worked an arithmetic problem, and discovered that the final figure was what it was supposed to be. However, my mind was not always so attentive to details. I was a daydreamer, carrying my fantasies into a world where everyone needed an expensive new watch, and every day was a walk on the dunes with the sunshine warming my cheeks.

The headmaster of our school was a strict taskmaster, insisting upon obedience and discipline without question. He had warned all the children not to step on the "blue stone," which was a small square stone slightly higher than the rest in the outer yard. I was not paying attention to his instructions and stepped on the stone. Instantly my face was smarting from a sharp slap on my cheek. I can still feel the shame of it, after all these years, for I don't believe the people at home had ever slapped my face. A color photoplate was impressed upon my mind, which has never faded. The tears covered my face, but I could see the girl who stood in front of me who wore a red dress and a white apron; there was a green door on the garden gate, and the colors all blended with the blazing eyes of Mr. Loran, the headmaster.

I couldn't wait to get home that day. Before I opened the door my cries had overpowered the sound of the bell, which announced any visitors to the shop.

Mama took me on her lap and comforted me; and when I had quieted, Papa held me in his arms as he did when I was a baby. I can still feel the sensation of safety as I put my head upon his shoulder. What a security to have a refuge when life is really hard!

Forty-five years passed after the blue-stone incident. The gestapo had arrested me, and I was being asked the location of the secret room in which I had hidden four Jews and two underground workers. I realized that if I told, it would mean prison and possibly death for the six people who were there, so I didn't tell. The interrogator slapped me on the face, and at the same moment I recalled the backyard of the school, the angry headmaster, and Mother and Father's comforting help.

"Lord Jesus, cover me!" I cried.

"If you mention that name, I'll murder you!" shouted the man. But his hand stopped in midair and he couldn't beat me any longer.

What a security to have a refuge when life is really hard!

In dat Vaderhuis (In That Father-house)

Our house was not very big, but it had wide open doors. I don't think that many guests who came to the Beje ever realized what a struggle it was to make both ends meet. As Mother said, "We must turn every penny twice before we spend it."

We didn't feel that we were poor, however, and indeed we weren't. The words "we can't afford it" were not a part of our thinking, because as children we knew something about the status of family finances, and didn't ask for what we knew was impossible.

Many lonesome people found a place with us, where there was music, humor, interesting conversations, and always room for one more at the oval dinner table. Oh, it's true, the soup may have been a bit watery when too many unexpected guests came, but it didn't really matter.

Mother loved guests. Her lovely blue eyes would brighten, and she would pat her dark hair into place when she knew we would be squeezing another visitor around our table—already bursting with four children, three aunts, herself, and Papa. With a flourish she would place a little box on the table, and spreading her arms wide, she would say to our visitor, "You are welcome in our house, and because we are grateful for your coming, we will add a penny to the blessing box for our missionaries."

Years afterwards on my trips around the world, when I have been dependent upon the hospitality of others, I believe that I have enjoyed the reward for the open doors and hearts of our home. Here on earth I have enjoyed a "house with many mansions."

I often think of that verse which says, "Cast thy bread upon the waters: for thou shalt find it after many days" (Ecclesiastes 11:1 KJV).

Corrie, Stand Still!

Although money was scarce, the outside world thought we were wealthy. Every member of the family dressed neatly and well. At least—almost everyone. Mother made most of our clothes, until the burden became too much, and Miss Anna van der Weyden, the seamstress, came in to help.

Clothes to me were just something to keep me covered and warm. The endless fittings for a new dress and the inevitable pricks from countless pins were torture to my restless body.

"Corrie, come here, dear," Mother would call in the tone I knew was meant to be another torturous session trying on clothes.

"If I don't finish this homework, Mama, Master Robyns will make me stand in the corner."

"Corrie!"

There was no escape. I knew if I didn't subject myself to trying on a new dress which Mama was making, that I would probably be assigned next time to Miss van der Weyden, and her clothes didn't fit as well as Mama's. The whole process was such a bore, and there was no way I could look like Nollie or Betsie anyhow. I just preferred to be me. However, I was a ten Boom and must not bring shame to the family name!

Mother had such a marvelous sense of humor, and having been a kindergarten teacher before her marriage, we profited by her practical knowledge of child psychology. She knew that praising my appearance would not provide me with motivation for my self-esteem. However, when she said, "Correman, you are such a bright girl . . . I'm sure Master Robyns calls on you often in class. You do want to look nice when you stand up to recite, don't you?" Then she would strike a responsive chord, for I was eager to learn and have recognition in school.

I stood still for Mama, but only briefly. There was so much to do, so many things to learn, so much to live. I had a built-in sense of urgency to cram all that life and love could offer into each precious day.

4

The Many Ages of Love

Children need the wisdom of their elders; the aging need the encouragement of a child's exuberance.

Wisdom and exuberance lived side by side in the Beje, a house filled with the varied personalities of the old and the young.

Tante Bep (Alone in the Crowd)

Children's nurses in the rich houses of Holland were very lonely. They were not at home in the kitchen with the servant girls (who thought the nurses had privileges which they didn't enjoy), and they were not at home in the drawing room with the master and mistress of the house. Consequently, they frequently became bitter with their circumstances of not belonging in any niche of society. Tante Bep was a children's nurse, going from job to job, and becoming more unhappy each year.

She was the oldest of Mother's sisters, and one of the reasons (I realize now) that my mother was very skilled in the art of tact. Mother usually had to steer a smooth course in our family with all of the aunts and their individual views on education and discipline; she knew how to bring the ship between the rocks.

When Tante Bep became too weak to work as a nurse, Father and Mother took her in. She had the same big, beautiful eyes like Mother, but the expression was very unhappy. She was quarrelsome about everything. There was the issue of the coffee, for instance. She told Tante Anna, "I'm the only one in this house who can make coffee." Now if there's one thing that was important in our house it was a good cup of coffee. Tante Anna would shift her apron around her ample waist, clear her throat with gusto and say, "Bep, if you think your coffee is so good, you may just take over all the cooking from now on."

"Anna," Mother would say with her soft smile and gentle persuasion, "we couldn't exist without your fine cooking—and Bep, I know your coffee is excellent, too; so perhaps you would like to make it your way on Tuesdays and Thursdays."

It was such a small house, it was impossible to avoid Tante Bep, but I tried because I didn't like to be compared to the Waller children. The last place she worked before coming to live with us was with the Wallers, and I thought they must have been angels who had their halos polished every day.

The Waller children were always neat. The Waller children never ran in the house. I didn't like to tell Tante Bep anything, because she might say, "The Waller children would never say such a thing."

Mother always soothed my insulted feelings by telling me, "Tante Bep complained about the Waller children when she was caring for them. Love her for what she is, Correman, and remember that she has had a very lonely sort of a life."

Tante Jans (That's That!)

"Corrie, close the door . . . my feet are cold and I'll be sick with all the drafts in this house."

Tante Jans was always concerned about her health, and made us very conscious of her needs. She had a diet which was different from the usual fare of the rest of the family; as a child, I sometimes thought it would be interesting to be sick and have my own trays of food and special attention.

Her rooms were special, too. Mother and Father had given

her more floor space than the rest of the family, because Tante Jans had a great deal of furniture to fill the rooms which she occupied upstairs.

Her husband had been a well-known minister in Rotterdam, and she had worked faithfully beside him in the church. They had no children, and it was a great loss in her life when he died before she was forty years old. After his death, it was clear that her place was to be in our house.

Tante Jans was not a woman to curl up with grief, and as soon as she had become established in her new quarters, she began all of her many activities which contributed to our buzzing household.

She was a poetess, an authoress, and an unusually good speaker. She started a monthly paper for girls, wrote books with a Gospel message, organized clubs for young women, and even began a club for soldiers.

One time Tante Jans swept into the house, pulling the scarf off her mouth, and proclaimed, "There are soldiers wandering around the streets of Haarlem with idle minds and mischievous thoughts. I am going to start a club for soldiers."

That's that! It was settled. When Tante Jans made one of her announcements, the wheels were set in motion. Before we knew what had happened our house began to look like a military installation. They would come alone or in pairs, young men who disliked the street life and were looking for the simple warmth of a home. One sergeant she met on a streetcar was a great musician. When he saw the harmonium which Tante Jans had against the wall of her room, he sat down and began to play, making the thin walls of the house quiver with each crescendo of volume.

Tante Jans folded her hands and listened intently to the talented soldier. She decided that Nollie and I should have him give us music lessons.

Even if we had not enjoyed music, we would have learned because Tante Jans decreed it. Soon I could play hymns well enough to join in the meetings and accompany the singing. It taught me at a very young age not to be self-conscious in the presence of men—although I don't think that was the intent of Tante Jans.

Some people have the gift of raising money by convincing others of the worth of a project, and this was one of Tante Jans's special talents. One afternoon she had a tea and invited some wealthy women she knew to come to her rooms. We scurried around rubbing her silver tea set until it glistened, and making sure everything was immaculate for the occasion.

I peeked out the window and watched the ladies arrive, swishing into the house with their long dresses underlined with full petticoats. How could they possibly walk and maneuver the narrow stairway with all those skirts? I had a hard time just keeping my feet in front of me! It must be a burden to be rich and have to dress in such fancy clothes, I thought.

Evidently Tante Jans was convincing, for in a short time she had enough money to build a military home. When it was finished and filled with soldiers, she went twice a week to give Bible studies.

Tante Jans didn't move with the times; she marched to her own beat. Her outspoken ideas on behavior, clothes, and theology were constant abrasives on the surface of our family relationships.

When I was a child, I thought Tante Jans was very rich, because she was a minister's widow and received a small, regular pension. Sometimes she would have an unexpected donation, and we would all share her joy. However, when she bought clothing for us it could be embarrassing—especially for Nollie and Betsie who had their own very distinctive tastes.

"Oh, dear," Betsie would say as she turned to give us the effect of a drab gray dress Tante Jans had given her. "Do you think she would mind if I put some lace around the neck—or maybe a pink sash at the waist?"

"Betsie, if you think that's bad, just look at this hat," Nollie would groan as she pulled a bonnet on backwards, sending us all into suppressed giggles. Tante Jans's taste in hats was somewhere between the style of a servant girl and that of a great-grandmother. Nollie was very fashion-conscious, and the gifts of stodgy clothes were a challenge to her ingenuity.

I didn't care about my appearance; I accepted all she gave me and consequently received the most hats and dresses. During the First World War most of Tante Jans's income stopped; it was dependent upon gifts of people who were having a financial struggle themselves. I remember she was surprised by an unexpected gift of fifty guilders (about eighteen dollars), and quickly gathered her muffler and umbrella to go shopping. When she returned, we thought something amazing must have happened, because she had forgotten to button her coat to the top. The sight of Tante Jans with face flushed and scarf loose was as uncommon as seeing the Queen riding in a streetcar!

"Come in everyone . . . I have something to show you." We all followed her into her room, and she spread her packages on the sofa, and began to distribute them with suppressed excitement. There was a warm blanket for Mother, a coat for me (black and shapeless, but practical), a blouse for Tante Anna, and cakes for the whole family. Any sweets were rare for us, reserved for birthdays and very special occasions.

I found out later that she had spent more than seventy guilders on us. I believe she was one of the richest persons I have known, for she knew how to give to others.

Tante Anna (Sheltering Apron)

Tante Anna, stocky, practical, unsentimental, was our substitute mother whenever Mother was too ill to care for us. She ruled over her little basement kitchen like one of Tante Jans's sergeants over his platoon. She was firm and hard working, but overflowing with love for Mother, Father, and all the children. When I was very young, I would stand beside her in our basement kitchen and lick the bowl of something she had been making. I watched the legs of the people passing by the kitchen window, for that was all we could see from beneath the street level. I began to wonder about all the people in the gigantic world outside.

"Tante Anna, where do babies come from?" I asked.

She stirred the *alle haphetzelfde* a bit and answered carefully, "Well, Corrie, when a baby is too small and weak to live in the cold world, there is a place underneath a mother's heart where it is kept warm and can grow, until it is strong enough to stand the cold in the big world."

I could understand that. It seemed like a very good plan of the Lord's.

My question answered in a simple manner, I went on to the more important matters of life, such as investigating with my finger the inside of another bowl. This one contained a special treat—*allusion,* which was a dessert made with stiffened egg whites and flavored with lemon and sugar. There was more air than substance, but good for a big family.

Tante Anna was a good cook, stretching a little far. She would cook a stew on the big, black coal stove until most of the vegetables all blended into each other. The *alle haphetzelfde* meant "every bite the same," and I know it was a real surprise and a treat when we encountered a bit of meat.

She had her club work, too, and her concern for others reached into the homes of the wealthy who employed servant girls. Every Wednesday and Sunday evening a group of them would come to a clubroom, and bring their sewing and embroidery work. Tante Anna taught them gospel songs and gave them a Bible study. When one of "her girls" went the wrong way Tante Anna became ill. Her face would become puffy and swell, and we didn't have to ask; we knew that she had received a piece of bad news.

"Tante Anna, who was it this time?" we would ask.

She would take her apron and try to hide her blotchy face. "It was Betty," she would say, dabbing at her eyes, "she wasn't strong enough in the Lord . . . she ran off with Hans . . . he's had two wives before this!" She would become as distressed as any mother would over a wayward child.

"Anna," Father would say, "you must not bear this yourself. Cast your worries upon the Lord."

Nollie (*Mijn Moedertje*)

Nollie was physically the strongest of the three girls in the family. I considered her my elder, although she was only a year and a half older than I. Even when she was a little child,

Corrie and Nollie (*mijn moedertje*).

she felt responsible for me; she was my *moedertje* (little mother). As a toddler, whenever she drank water she brought a cup for me, too. I had to drink even if I wasn't thirsty. After all, Nollie knew best. I was shy and she was not; she voiced her needs and views. I waited.

One time, when we were very young, Nollie and I were out for a walk, when a man on a bicycle knocked us down right in front of our house. Covered with mud and shocked, we ran into the sitting room, loudly declaring our presence.

Nollie screamed and everyone came running, brushing her hair out of her eyes, wiping off the dirt, and kissing away the tears. I stood in the corner, watching all the commotion and wondering when I should take my turn screaming—after Nollie was through, of course. I knew my time to be comforted would come.

Suddenly Mother said, *"Hemeltje!* [Little Heaven!] Come look at Corrie."

Everyone stopped, and for the first time realized that I was standing in the corner of the room, big tears making muddy rivers down my cheeks. Finally I was given the attention of the grown-ups.

The little alley beside our house was the locale of many events in our lives. There wasn't much room for playing in our overcrowded house, so the alley was our yard, our recreation room, and our schoolhouse of life. Once Nollie met a little boy named Sammy Staal. I think there must have been something wrong with his heart, for his skin had a bluish color and his nose was always red. He was unable to walk, and propelled himself in a wheelchair. Nollie made friends with him, and encouraged by Mother, she would push him for hours and hours while the rest of the children were playing active games. When he died, Nollie was heartbroken.

Nollie's grief was probably a shared feeling. Even when we were very young, we knew that our problems were never too small for the grown-ups; there were many ways and many ages of love under one Dutch roof.

5

Winking Angels

Secrets are for children, and promises are like soap bubbles—easy to make, easy to break. The one time I tried to keep a secret from Mama, my little deception was uncovered. I talked in my sleep.

I was very young, perhaps eight or nine, and very flattered that Richard would ask me to go for a walk through the dunes. He was the nephew of our minister, and quite grown-up—a teenager.

However, I was not prepared for an act of boyish curiosity which surprised and shamed me at the same time. We had reached a valley where we could not be seen, and suddenly he pulled me close to him and started to do very strange things. Even without previous warnings from protective parents, I knew this was wrong.

I pulled away from him, flushing with childish indignation, and stamped my foot, "Richard, you stop that. Mama would think that's dirty!"

Richard looked frightened, but defiant. "She isn't here . . . and you mustn't tell."

"Mama isn't here, but Jesus is and I'm sure He doesn't think it's right."

Richard was defeated. He stopped immediately and said, "Promise me never to tell anyone what I tried to do, especially your mother?"

I thought this over for a while. After all, he was Richard, and a very important person in my eyes.

"Well, I guess so . . . I promise."

As we walked back home, he told me some very nice stories and I forgot about the incident.

At least I thought I forgot about it!

The next day I was ill and had a fever. I talked about the walk on the dunes, but wasn't conscious of what I had said. After the fever was gone, Mama asked me what had happened with Richard.

"A promise is a promise, Mama, and I said I wouldn't tell anybody in the world."

"Correman, never forget that Jesus is always with you. Every morning I ask Him to keep you and all of my children within His constant care. In the evening, I thank Him that He sent His angels to guard you. Now you and I will pray together."

I remember Mother folded her soft hands around mine when she prayed. I thought how wonderful it was that she asked Jesus to guard me. She prayed, "Thank You, Jesus, that You never leave my Correman alone . . . thank You that You protected her during her walk on the dunes. Please lay Your hand on Richard . . . show him how wrong he was and that You are willing to make him a good clean boy."

How did she know about Richard? I wondered if mothers know everything. Oh, well, never mind . . . Jesus knows, Mama knows, and everything is all right.

Dutch Mischief-Makers

I was no little angel. *Mischief* was my middle name, and Dot, my cousin and best friend, was my willing partner. Her father, Uncle Arnold, was the usher, or verger, of St. Bavo's, the magnificent Gothic cathedral which dominates the center of Haarlem. Its cavernous interior provided endless hours of imaginary play. In the banks (or pews) with their enclosed rows

of seats, shut off from the aisles by half-doors, a child could
have a private house. We could be pirates, hiding in our caves,
or storekeepers in our offices; we could run a school or own a
sweet shop.

The pulpit was out of bounds. We were not allowed to go
there; that wasn't proper, or respectful. It seemed quite awe-
some to a small child, because the chair in the pulpit doesn't
stand on the ground. It is held up by the bronze wings of an
eagle. The font in front of the pulpit is supported by three
brass snakes, and that was enough to keep us away without
being told.

Our voices would echo in the stone interior, adding intrigue
to our games. Sometimes Uncle Arnold would have to hush our
exuberance.

"Children, children, there are graves beneath our feet. Step
softly."

The position of usher carried the privilege of living within
the cathedral grounds. Uncle Arnold's family had a cozy little
house just off the side entrance to the church. I always loved
going in through the narrow passageway surrounded by beautiful blue Dutch tiles.

Living within the cathedral didn't make Dot any holier.
If I didn't dream up a prank, she would.

We were in the same grade in school and usually walked
together to our classes. I was comfortable with Dot, because we
were on the same level of academic achievement, which was
toward the bottom of the class. Whenever we had difficulty with
our homework we asked Josien van Paassen to help us. She was
not only bright but also owned a bicycle. A winning combination. Her father was a minister with a regular monthly income,
but the earnings of a watchmaker went up and down like the
weights on the grandfather clock.

One morning Dot called for me on the way to school, and
she was unusually excited. "Corrie, come here, look what I
found."

She handed me a dime which was broken in half; the coin
had probably been run over by a carriage, and the two pieces
were wedged on the cobblestones just waiting for a little girl

to pick them up. A dime was a great deal of money to us; it could buy ten pieces of candy at the sweet shop on the Begyne-straat. Such a rare and wonderful treat!

We skipped off to school, neither one of us admitting that we thought we were going to do anything wrong, and ordered our candies from the jolly lady who owned the shop. Dot slipped the two parts of the dime to me and I placed them on the counter, then made a very fast retreat out the door. We were running toward school, when we heard the bell of the shop door ring and the owner call, "Girls . . . girls . . . come back . . . !"

I grabbed Dot's hand and we ran a little faster, my feet having their usual problem of keeping up with my own momentum. We felt so guilty and for weeks avoided going by the candy store. The candy didn't taste very good, either, and in later years when I read this Proverb I thought about that childish caper. "Bread obtained by falsehood is sweet to a man, But afterward his mouth will be filled with gravel" (Proverbs 20:17). Can candy really taste like gravel?

Another time Dot and I made some solid snowballs and put them in our pockets. It was so cold, they didn't melt but formed hard balls just the right size for mittened hands to grasp and throw. We were walking through the Kruisstraat behind three dignified men, who were loudly discussing their problems. I winked at Dot and we reached into our pockets, drew out our ammunition, took aim, and fired. The top hats flew into the snowy streets, and two sweet little girls raced to pick them up.

"Here you are, sir," I said with a serious face and very polite demeanor, as I brushed the snow carefully off the hat. Dot picked up the second hat and handed it to one gentleman who had a very bald, cold head. He fitted the hat on his head and said, "Thank you, young ladies," as he looked around to see who the rascals were who committed such a crime.

Hats Off

Not all my episodes with hats went unpunished, however. The director of our school was a very strict man, not the type of person who would tolerate misbehavior from his students. Father had helped Mr. van Lyden start the Christian educational institution, and because of this assistance we didn't pay to attend it, a fact which was a great help to the ten Boom family. When the school was new, many of the disciplinary problem children from other areas were sent there, and several times Mr. van Lyden had to send them back to the schools they had attended previously.

I was shocked when a student was expelled. Just imagine how humiliating it was for the parents to have their child sent away from school for bad behavior!

I must have been about ten years old when this occurred. I sat at my desk, gazing out the window, watching the wind swirl the dust on the playground. I was thinking about the new hat Tante Jans had given me, a large blue and white sailor, which I hated just because it was a hat. The teacher stepped out of the room and an idea flashed into my mind.

"Listen, everyone," I said to the class, "I have a brilliant idea. Exactly at two o'clock we'll all put on our hats or caps. We can smuggle them under the desks so Mr. van Ree won't see them. I've got a watch and I'll give the sign."

The room of sixty ten-year-olds crackled with excitement, and I was the leader. The fact that I had a watch made me very important, because I was the only one in the class who had one.

Two o'clock arrived and the classroom was very quiet. We were working our arithmetic problems in silence, and the teacher looked from one to another, distrusting our unusually good behavior.

I was sitting toward the front of the class and, after giving the signal, I took my hat from under the desk and put it on. I didn't hear a thing in back of me. I looked around, and to my horror saw that no one else had the nerve to follow my example, except Jan Vixeboxe who sat way in back of the room. When my eyes returned to the teacher, he was staring right at me, furiously glaring from humorless eyes. There was terror in the atmosphere.

"Go to the headmaster at once, Corrie ten Boom!" he commanded.

Oh, no, not the headmaster! That was Mr. van Lyden, and he expelled students for infraction of the rules.

I slipped from behind my desk, pulling off my hat as I left the room. In the hallway I opened the coat closet and ducked in, hiding myself in a dark corner behind the coats. I don't know how many miserable hours I spent there, but it seemed like an eternity before the bell rang, and I ran out ahead of the rest of the students.

I expected to be dismissed, just as the problem pupils from other schools had been. I thought of all the shame I would bring to Mama and Papa, of all they would have to go through because of my misdeed. How I loved them! I thought of all the care they had given me, of the difficulties we had as a result of sickness and lack of money. We were such a close-knit family that we always shared joys and sorrows, and now this! Dismissed from the school my father had helped organize!

At the supper table that night I was so quiet Mama thought I was sick. I went upstairs early and crept into bed, pulling the comforter under my chin. I told Nollie everything that had happened.

"Why don't you ask forgiveness of God?" she suggested.

"I've already done that . . . but do you think He will arrange it so that I won't be sent away from school?"

I asked Nollie the deep questions which were puzzling me, because she was almost twelve! Certainly she would know all the answers.

"I don't know," Nollie replied, "but do you remember that boring Psalm that Papa read at the table, where every sixth or seventh verse were the same words? '. . . Then they cried unto the Lord in their trouble, and he saved them out of their distresses' " (Psalms 107 KJV).

For the first time since the hats-off incident I began to cheer up. "Why couldn't we do the same?"

We "cried unto the Lord" and then fell asleep. The next morning Nollie shook me awake and told me her wonderful idea. We had a little monthly missionary magazine that I delivered to several people as my special work in evangelizing the world. Mr. van Lyden was one of the subscribers. Nollie suggested, "You must manage in some way to go to the headmaster, and personally bring him the mission magazine for this month. It can't do any harm, and perhaps it will do some good."

That morning, with my heart pounding right through my best school dress and a very pious expression on my face, I went to the headmaster's room and handed him the paper. He looked at it and then at me. The pause took a hundred years and the silence hurt my ears. He didn't have much of a sense of humor, but I believe the corners of his mouth turned up just a little bit.

He cleared his throat, tapped the desk with his pencil, and said, "Corrie ten Boom, I don't think you behaved as a very good Christian girl yesterday."

That was all I ever heard about my crime. The Lord saved me from my distress.

Mice in the Manuscript

When I was about twelve, I decided that I wanted to be a writer. I curled up on my bed, pad of paper on my lap, and wove a wonderful fantasy about the adventures of Nollie, Josien, Dot, and all of Dot's brothers and sisters on a holiday without our parents. It was a beautiful story, filled with more adventure than Dickens, and more vivid character sketches than Louisa May Alcott. How famous I would be!

Betsie shattered my dreams. She came into the room and asked, "What's that?"

It seemed quite obvious to me. "It's a book I'm writing," I answered as smugly as a sister seven years younger could reply to the ridiculous question of a grown-up.

Betsie seldom voiced any words of discouragement, but this time she said, "How foolish . . . you can't write a book."

I just won't show anyone my book anymore, I thought. So I hid it in the attic and forgot the priceless manuscript for several months.

When I remembered later to take the papers out of their secret niche, there was only one-tenth of this potential best seller left. The rest was eaten by the mice. I was so disappointed that I decided never to write a book again.

The Shadow of His Wings

My security was assured in many ways as a child. Every night I would go to the door of my room in my nightie and call out, "Papa, I'm ready for bed." He would come to my room and pray with me before I went to sleep. I can remember that he always took time with us, and he would tuck the blankets around my shoulders very carefully, with his own characteristic precision. Then he would put his hand gently on my face and say, "Sleep well, Corrie . . . I love you."

I would be very, very still, because I thought that if I moved I might lose the touch of his hand; I wanted to feel it until I fell asleep.

Many years later in a concentration camp in Germany, I sometimes remembered the feeling of my father's hand on my face. When I was lying beside Betsie on a wretched, dirty mattress in that dehumanizing prison, I would say, "Oh, Lord, let me feel Your hand upon me . . . may I creep under the shadow of Your wings."

In the midst of that suffering was my heavenly Father's security.

Reach As High As You Can

My desire to please my papa was one of the basic motivations of my life. I remember when I was walking home from school, there was a very dirty wall I passed every day. It was full of flies, and during the warm weather one of my games was to run my hand along the wall and try to catch a fly. When the challenge had been met, I would release it and try for the next catch.

One day when I was busy with this messy game I heard a familiar voice behind me, "Now isn't this a joy to meet my youngest daughter here on the street."

I was suddenly very embarrassed about how dirty I was, for Papa was so immaculate and well dressed that I didn't dare put my hand in his. He never mentioned my appearance, just walked along chatting about the visit to Mrs. de Vries and his talk with the servant girl about the Lord, until we arrived inside the Beje.

"I'm home, Cor," he'd call to Mama. Then he turned to me and said, "And I know, Corrie, that you're going to wash your hands before you see your mother."

Such a small thing, but I remember the shame of being so dirty in Papa's presence.

We were always challenged to do our best. When Papa took a watch apart and put it back together again, it was a task he performed without regard to the owner's social status or wealth. He taught us that it wasn't important what you think, or even what other people think, but what God thinks about the job you have done.

When Nollie and I were teenagers, we decided to take sewing lessons. I made a blouse; it was a very careless job, with crooked seams and poorly fitted sleeves. I pulled it on, knowing that I looked very sloppy but not really caring much until I saw Papa's face. "Corrie, the servant girl may be able to teach you how to scrub a floor, but your mother should teach you how to sew. When you spend your time and money on making something, it should be your best effort."

Achievement and honesty were such basic ingredients in Papa's personality that there were times when we had to hide the giggles he disliked so much. One of the stories Mama told about him was, "My husband is so honest that when the children were babies, he wouldn't allow me to give them a pacifier, no matter how loud or how long they cried. He would say, 'They think they are getting a drink. That is fooling a child to put something in her mouth which is a lie.' "

Mama would sigh with amused resignation and say, "So my babies never had a pacifier, because my husband is so honest."

Papa was honest about pain, too. Whenever we had to go to a dentist or a doctor, Papa would come along to comfort us. However, he would never say that we would not have pain. He said that if we had to have a tooth filled or pulled, that we must be brave and strong. Whenever it was possible, he went with us. Holding his hand gave us courage. If the doctor did need his assistance, his strong hands kept our hands or head from moving.

Perhaps it is wrong to tell this today—in view of the permissive way in which many children are being raised—but we were disciplined without spanking. I cannot remember being paddled as a child, but there was no doubt in our family that we were to obey Father. His will was law and we all knew it.

We never spoke about the "line of authority" in our home—it was simply understood. Father didn't have to stand up and say, "I'm the head of this family!" He just was. We never felt any desire to have it any other way, because the love and security of all our relationships were built upon the established fact that God was always with us, and He had appointed Casper ten Boom in charge of the mansion in Haarlem called the Beje.

6

Around the Oval Table

Can a piece of furniture be important? The oval table in our dining room was the gathering place for hopes and dreams, the listening place for prayers and petitions, and the loving place for joy and laughter.

But Sunday it was something more—it was the special place for family and friends.

Sunday was an important day for us; it was a day when everything—from the clothes we wore to the spoons we used—was distinctive. My Sunday dress was the new one I received for Christmas, so I seldom had a choice about what I would wear to church. Tante Anna could work magic with that dress, adding a colored sash or a ribbon in a way that improved my rather careless appearance. It was another of her small gifts of service which said, "I care."

When we were ready for church, Father would lead the way to St. Bavo's while we trailed along, trying not to scuff our shoes or muss our Sunday outfits.

After church it was good to go home, especially when the weather was chilly, for St. Bavo's was unheated, and there were days when my teeth would chatter through the entire service.

At home I would help with the Sunday dinner, first by

smoothing a beautiful white cloth over the oval table. I tried to do this carefully, because I knew that Betsie wanted it to hang evenly, and it was a great desire of mine to meet her standards. Everything about Betsie was neat and I was . . . oh, well—just Corrie.

"Good work, Corrie," she would say, and that was all I needed to encourage me for the rest of the day.

The delicate china, which had been brought from Indonesia by father's older sister, Tante Toos, and Tante Jans's ornate silver service—a gift from wealthy members of her husband's church—were placed on the table. Then Tante Anna would emerge from the kitchen, wiping her hands on the generous apron she used to cover her black silk dress, and ring a little bell.

"Come to dinner, everyone."

When we were seated, Father would remove his fresh Sunday napkin from its holder, place it carefully on his lap, and bow his head.

"Lord, we thank You for this beautiful Lord's Day and for this family. Bless this food, bless our Queen, and let soon come the day that Jesus, Your beloved Son, comes on the clouds of heaven. *Amen.*"

Our table talk on Sunday sometimes centered around the sermon we had heard, but usually Father was cautious not to say too much. He attended the cathedral near our home because he felt that God had called him to that place, but he didn't hold any position in the church. His views were not accepted by the liberal thinkers who were in positions of leadership.

Conversations around the dinner table were lively because we all had stories or experiences we wanted to share. I believe that the great enjoyment of a family eating together is having this time when each person can be heard.

Father had a special talent in directing our talks so that no one would feel left out. We loved to tell personal stories, but were taught to laugh at ourselves, not to make fun of others.

I remember one time when Nollie was telling about a painting she had done in school.

"I thought the drawing was rather good," Nollie said, "but

when Mr. van Arkel walked over to my desk, he held up my picture and looked at it one way and then another, scowling all the time."

"Maybe he just wanted to get a better view," Betsie offered.

"I'm afraid that wasn't his reason," Nollie answered.

(Studies were important in our family, so each one of us received special attention when we talked about school.)

"What did Mr. van Arkel say, Nollie?" Mother asked.

"He said, 'Do you know of which Proverb your drawing reminds me, Nollie ten Boom?' "

"I told him *'Honi soit qui mal y pense.'* [Disgraced is he who thinks wrong of it.] It's from a motto on a badge of knighthood. Boy, did Mr. van Arkel laugh!"

Nollie's eyes twinkled when she told the story. Father really enjoyed a good joke, as long as the girls didn't giggle. Laughter he loved, but giggling was *verboden.*

On Sunday afternoons we frequently had visitors who would stop for a cup of tea and conversation. Sometimes we would go for a walk, but we didn't study, sew, or work on the Lord's Day. The only work allowed was winding the watches which were in the shop for repair.

Father said, "Even on Sunday, I must milk my cows."

Father's Friends

Fellowship around the oval table was more than just a family affair. Throughout the years there were many people, young and old, rich and poor, who contributed so much to the richness of my childhood. I loved to have some of Father's friends visit in our home, because they laughed a lot and always told wonderful stories.

When Father was a young man in Amsterdam he worked in a mission called *Heil des Volks,* which was in a very poor part of the city. There were three other men who gave their time and energy to this particular outreach and they all became fast friends.

The four men would meet often, sharing their burdens and triumphs, studying the Bible together, and discussing many topics of interest. As a child, I was always happy when they

came to our house; it was a time when I loved to listen to the
conversations of these great friends and learn from their experiences. The children were welcome to stay during their discussions, and encouraged to participate if we had something we
wanted to ask. I can still recall the fragrant mixture of cologne
and good Dutch cigars which lingered in the room.

Frits Vermeer was a rather round Dutchman who loved to
joke. He was "Uncle Frits" to us, just as the other good friends
were called Uncle Dirk and Uncle Hendrik.

One of the first things Father would do when his friends
arrived was to bring out the box of cigars from its place in the
desk where the bulky ledger of the shop was kept. From his
pocket, he would take the special cigar clipper which had keys
for winding the clocks on the other side. It was a very important
tool, and many children over a span of half a century sat on his
lap and played with it.

Uncle Hendrik was considered the theologian of the group,
and was constantly being challenged for a Bible verse to meet
some situation or problem. He was seldom at a loss when asked
to quote something appropriate for the occasion.

Uncle Dirk, the fourth member of the group, was the only
one who wasn't married. However, he loved children very much
and was able to express that love in a special way.

On one occasion, when Father's friends were discussing their
concerns, Uncle Dirk was anxious to tell about an orphanage
where he was on the board of directors. I sat up and listened
carefully, because children without parents bothered me so
much. I thought how terrible it would be not to have the love
of a mother and father.

"I decided to become the father of the orphanage," Uncle
Dirk announced. "I have been on the board of directors, argu-
ing for better conditions for those poor children, but I have
not seen any positive results. I must get in there and work
myself."

Father was delighted. "Dirk, this is certainly the leading of
the Lord for you. He has not given you a wife, but He is going
to bless you with many, many children. We will pray about it."

Father would begin to pray with his friends in an attitude

which was so easy and natural that the conversation never seemed to stop; it would flow easily from friend to friend to the Lord.

Many times through the years I remember the wonderful moments I had listened to the stories and experiences of Father's friends. There is a Proverb which says, "Do not forsake your own friend or your father's friend . . ." (Proverbs 27:10). I have often thought how wise that is.

Bible Study Was a Game

With the dishes cleared off and kitchen duties accomplished, the oval table could be turned into a place for games. We didn't play cards (for that was considered a form of gambling), but we had a lasting enjoyment in the type of games which taught us something.

Different languages were introduced as a game, not as a forced study. When I was in the fourth grade, we began to learn French. As I remember, I loved the melodious sounds of this beautiful language, but it was and remained a difficult language for me. The next year I started English, which was easier but I wondered as I struggled with all the different English meanings for words if I would ever go to England or America and have an opportunity to use the language.

Father wanted me to learn English well, and he gave me a little Sunday-school booklet in English which was called "There's No Place Like Home." I read it over and over again.

The greatest fun in language-learning came during our Bible study. The entire family would take part, each one of us having a Bible in a different language. Willem usually had the original in Hebrew and Greek; I would have the English; Mother the Dutch; Nollie the French; and Betsie or Father, German. It was a special and joyous time for us.

Father would begin by asking what John 3:16 was in English. I would answer from my English Bible, Mother from her Dutch Bible, and Betsie would reply in German.

When I was so young, it didn't seem possible that Betsie would ever have a chance to use a Bible verse in German. We didn't know any Germans then! However, God uses such seemingly insignificant ways to prepare us for the plan He has for our lives. Over forty years later, in a concentration camp in Germany, Betsie was able to use that verse—and many more— to speak to the prisoners and the guards about God's love.

When Father Prayed . . .

Every room in our house heard our prayers, but the oval table probably experienced more conversations with the Lord than other places. Praying was never an embarrassment for us, whether it was with the family together or when a stranger came in. Father prayed because he had a good Friend to talk over the problems of the day; he prayed because he had a direct connection with his Maker when he had a concern; he prayed because there was so much for which he wanted to thank God.

When Father talked with the Lord it was serious, but un-pretentious. He talked to Someone he knew. Once we had a minister in our house, and when his visit was over, Father prayed, "Thank You, Lord, for a good day. We hope everyone goes together in the same way."

The minister left with a puzzled expression on his face. Could this be the Casper ten Boom so many of his parishioners told him had such a deep understanding of God's Word?

Father always prayed before and after each meal. He included two things in his prayer: the Queen and the Second Coming of Jesus Christ.

The knowledge and anticipation of the return of Jesus Christ was given to me by Father during one of the quiet, thoughtful times before I went to sleep as a small child. As for the Queen— patriotism and loyalty were an accepted way of thinking in our house, as it was in most Dutch homes. However, I never thought that the prayers of the little ten Boom girl would be answered in such unusual ways.

Me? A Guest of the Queen? Not Me!

It was the year 1956, more than half a century after I first heard Father pray for the Queen. I was in Formosa with Dr. Bob

Pierce, a man whose outreach of love and concern has spread throughout the world. He said to me one day, "Corrie, I believe it would be a good idea for you to talk with the Queen of your country."

Bob is an American, and I forgave him for not understanding about proper protocol with members of royalty. How ridiculous, I thought.

"Bob, you don't know what you're saying . . . I can't go see the Queen."

He looked at me gently and said, "Just pray about it." And so I did.

Wilhelmina had been Queen through two world wars; her reign had spanned two generations, and now she had abdicated and given the position of monarchy to her only daughter, who is our Queen Juliana. Wilhelmina chose to have the title of *Princess* from that moment on.

When I was back in my homeland, I wrote to Princess Wilhelmina, and said that I would like to meet her and bring greetings from Bob Pierce and World Vision International. The day after my letter was delivered the Princess sent her car to pick me up.

I sat in the back seat of the limousine, enjoying every kilometer from Haarlem to *Het Loo Apeldoorn*, where her palace was.

Wouldn't Father have loved this, I thought. *All those years he prayed for the Queen and here is his daughter, Corrie, having a visit with Princess Wilhelmina herself!*

One amazing thing after another happened. I was given the opportunity of speaking with the Queen and meeting all the people in the palace. After a few hours I had to tell Princess Wilhelmina that I had to leave for some meetings that were planned in Germany.

She looked at me and said, "I expected you to stay several weeks here, and you're just staying a few hours. Why are you going to Germany?"

The war had been over for more than ten years, but its memories were still vivid to many Hollanders.

"I must go to Germany, Your Highness, because God has called me to tell them of His love and forgiveness."

She dismissed what I was saying with a wave of her hand, but later when I returned once more to Holland she sent word for me to come and stay in the palace for a longer time. I was allowed on that visit one hour each evening with Princess Wilhelmina. She said, "I'm too old for too much, so we may either eat together or talk for an hour." I chose the last part, and had my meals with her lady-in-waiting afterwards. Princess Wilhelmina knew her Bible very well, and we enjoyed those hours in her lovely private chamber. She gave me the opportunity to tell her of the miracle God had worked in my life to forgive my enemies.

I believe that in some way something of Father's prayers many, many years before were answered when God allowed the daughter of the watchmaker to carry His message of love to the Queen.

I had a happy time of fellowship with many people in the palace. I had personal contact with most of them when we talked about the most important Person, our Lord Jesus Christ. But the happiest moments of each day were the hours with that great lady who had reigned over our little country in a time when two world wars had wounded Europe.

7

Seventeen, and
So Much to Learn

When Betsie told a story, she wove threads of brilliant color
through the word pictures she created. When she moved into
a room, or dressed for a meeting, it was with a special flair. She
knew *levenskunst* (the art of living)!

I wasn't what people would call a "mature" teenager. I was
a tomboy during my adolescence—not a "young lady." However,
I loved imitating and wanted to learn, but it didn't seem possible to me that I would ever have those soft qualities of
womanhood which were so natural to my older sister.

Betsie taught me many things, and one of them was how to
tell a story. She had a Sunday-school class for many years, starting to teach when she was seventeen. She loved her pupils, and
the little gifts and adoring glances she had from those boys and
girls proved that her love was returned many times. One day
she said to me, "Corrie, you must take a class, too."

"What can I teach?" I asked, thinking how embarrassed I
would be if someone asked me a question I couldn't answer.
There was so much I didn't understand, especially all those
Kings and Judges and battles in the Old Testament.

Betsie's answer was, "Try it! Tell the story of the feeding
of the five thousand."

Now there was a story I knew! So I went with her to her class, believing this was a very simple assignment. What an embarrassment! How inadequate I felt when I finished the story in five minutes. The class was thirty minutes long and I didn't know how to fill the remaining time. Betsie took over and I listened with amazement as she told the same story over to a spellbound class of kids.

I was rather discouraged; I didn't know how to tell a story, but after that experience I was determined to learn. As I listened to Betsie I realized that you must weave a tale, leading your listeners on a word journey.

A girl friend of mine, Mina, was a teacher in a Christian school and she promised to help me. We asked permission of the director of the school to allow me to give the Bible story in her class every Monday morning. They were pretty drab at first, but gradually I began to learn how to add those imaginative touches which made them more interesting.

I used the technique of describing one picture after another, leading my little class through the art gallery of the Bible. When I told the story of the feeding of the five thousand again, we visualized Jesus with all the people sitting on the grass around Him. We would look at these people individually, imagining where they lived, what sort of problems they had, and what they might be thinking about this Man with the divine love in His eyes. The next picture is of Jesus and His followers, the disciples, talking about how the tired, hungry people were going to be fed. There was no bakery or fish market within sight, but there was an obvious need for food. The blue waters of the Galilee reflected the surrounding green and brown hills, and the luxuriant grass where the people sat to listen to Jesus was pressed to the ground by the crowd.

Then I would carry my listeners with me to the climax, as Jesus took the five loaves and two fish offered Him by a boy who had gone shopping for his mother, and ". . . looking up toward heaven, He blessed the food and broke the loaves and He kept giving them to the disciples to set before them; He divided up the two fish among them all. And they all ate and were satisfied" (Mark 6:41, 42).

"What a feast we have when we believe Jesus Christ!" I would end.

I had no idea how valuable this lesson was going to be in later life. If Betsie had told me that someday I would be speaking before thousands of people, I'm sure that the fear of such a thing would have silenced my clumsy efforts at storytelling immediately.

From Bach With Love

Music was as much a part of my young life as television is to the children of today. Mother and Tante Anna had taught kindergarten, and I can remember their singing to me the little songs they taught to their schoolchildren. When I was old enough to sit at the organ called the harmonium and pump the pedals with my feet, Tante Jans had arranged for one of her military visitors to give Nollie and me music instruction.

We loved to sing in our house. Nollie had a rich soprano voice, Willem sang tenor, and I was the alto when we learned to sing the Bach chorale *"Seid froh die Weil."* I grew up loving Bach.

One time Father called us together and said, "We're going to St. Bavo's tomorrow evening for a great treat!"

I couldn't imagine anything that could be better than some of the concerts we had already enjoyed at Uncle Arnold's church. Because of Uncle Arnold's position as caretaker, we were given special permission to listen to the concerts, sitting on the bench beside the door which separated his home from the main sanctuary. Only the people who had money could afford to attend these fine concerts, and without Uncle Arnold, all the members of the ten Boom family would seldom have been able to enjoy such riches.

"Wear your warm clothes," Mama warned, as we were getting ready for the mysterious treat.

St. Bavo's was a vast, unheated building with footwarmers for those who could afford to pay, and a hard wooden bench with cold stone at our backs for Uncle Arnold's relatives.

We all lined up, excited over the anticipation of Father's

"great treat," and went to the cathedral, by-passing the front entrance and going in the side door to our own special reserved seats. The smell of moisture and dust, smoldering gas lamps, and the burning coals in the footwarmers was so familiar, and the excitement began to build. We sat down, with Father wrapping a wool blanket around Mother and placing a pillow at her back to make her more comfortable.

A wiry man with unruly gray hair and a drooping mustache passed us before going upstairs to the world-famous pipe organ. I had explored the area where this impressive organ stood and wondered how anyone could learn to play on so many manuals with sixty-eight stops. We had been told that Mozart played that organ when he was only ten years old.

We soon knew why the evening was going to be such a treat. I held my breath as Albert Schweitzer began playing a Bach prelude. He was an authority on organ building, and an organist who could fill the cathedral with exquisite beauty. During the day St. Bavo's was a composition in gray, inside and out, but in the evening—with the gas lamps giving a Rembrandtesque light, the pillars pointing upwards in a mysterious glow—the atmosphere of harmony was heaven. I thought eternity must contain this kind of beauty.

Albert Schweitzer was a German philosopher, physician, writer, and theologian. He had gone to Africa as a medical missionary and established a hospital and a leper colony. As his fame grew throughout the world, I often thought of the first time I heard him interpret Bach, and how much Father's treat contributed to my lifetime love of music.

Impatient to Learn Patience

We are not born with patience, and I believe God began to teach me something of what this means when I was in my seventeenth year. Because I was the youngest of the family, I remained childlike for a long time. I loved life intensely, charged with the desire to cram every available experience into each day. Then came a terrible blow which depressed me so severely, I thought I wouldn't survive.

For some weeks I had a slight fever. For a time I managed to disguise how I felt, but soon Mama began to see my listless attitude and called the doctor. He probed and tapped, listened and questioned, and then told me I had tuberculosis.

Death sentence! *So young,* I thought . . . *why would God want me with Him when there was so much for me to do on earth?*

"You must go to bed, Corrie, until the fever is gone," the doctor pronounced.

In those days tuberculosis was as fearful as cancer is now. I cried and went upstairs slowly, not looking back. It was the middle of the day and it seemed strange to undress and go to bed!

I cried to the Lord, "Why must I be ill, Lord? I will live! I will be healthy!" It took many days before I could surrender and accept the situation. I surely had to learn what it says in Colossians:

We pray that you will be strengthened from God's bound-less resources, so that you will find yourselves able to pass through any experience and endure it with courage. You will even be able to thank God in the midst of pain and distress . . . .

1:11, 12 PHILLIPS

Through my tears and anger, I would thank Him, but I couldn't understand why He wanted me to lie in bed, imprisoned by the walls of my little room.

At first many visitors came upstairs, but after several months had passed, some people forgot me. I began to feel more self-pity and rebellion, but I prayed every day for peace in my heart and finally the moment came when I could say, "Yes, Lord, You know best."

At that time Willem was a theological student at the University of Leiden. He was going to have an examination in church history, and often came home on weekends.

"I get things in my head if I teach them. How about it, Corrie, if I give you some books will you study them?"

It was not the first time I had to assist him in that way. To earn some money in his college time, he gave lessons in Latin to a boy who was a very unwilling pupil. Every morning from seven until eight o'clock he taught him, and I joined the two of them. If the boy didn't listen and was absolutely uncooperative, then Willem taught me Latin. I enjoyed those lessons, and knew that my brother was a good teacher.

I gained a great love for church history during those months of confinement, and it took my thoughts away from my illness.

The doctor did not visit me much; rest was the only cure he knew, and he told the family not to allow me to get out of bed until there was no sign of a fever. One day he passed my room after visiting Tante Bep, who was very old and feeble, and I called him.

"Doctor, I have a pain in my abdomen. It's right here," I said, pressing my fist on my right side.

He examined me and found an appendix infection, which was probably the cause of my fever all that time. I don't think anyone has ever been so happy with appendicitis! After five months of confinement I left my bed, had a minor operation, and returned to the wonderful outside world.

In the World, But Not of It

Until that time in my life the outside world was very small. It consisted of the streets and alleys of Haarlem, with only brief excursions with Father to Amsterdam, or an occasional visit to a neighboring village to visit friends.

I began to want to be somebody outside the protection of the Beje—to learn about the world that existed away from the Barteljoristraat. I didn't dream that I could see some of the countries and people that I read about in my geography book, but at least I wanted to experience life outside the shop.

Was I wrong? I struggled with this ambition and decided to ask my Bible teacher, Mrs. van Lennep, who was a very understanding woman who counseled well. She said, "Corrie, it's very natural for you to feel the way you do. You can do something in the world through the power of the Lord."

The first thing I did was launch into an intensive study of many subjects. I received diplomas in home economics, child care, needlepoint, and others. It proved to be a good background for my first job.

My opportunity came to be "out in the world." I heard about a job from one of the girls at school. The Bruins, who had a magnificent home, needed an *au paire* for their little girl. This position was a combination governess and companion. I knew this was what Tante Bep had done in her youth—and she had become a lonely and rather dour old woman—but this didn't quench my original enthusiasm for what I thought would be a new adventure in living.

Father and Mother gave their permission, and I packed my few clothes in a little suitcase and left with great anticipation for Zandvoort, a village by the sea, about ten miles from Haarlem.

The contrast between my homelife and my new job began with my first glimpse of the home. It was so big! How could just one family live in a house that size?

As I began my job, I tried very hard to please the entire family. At home I had always known fun and laughter, with a large dose of love and affection. Out in the world it wasn't the same. For the first time I was faced with a new way of thinking, a different kind of family life than I had ever experienced.

If this was the way to "be somebody," I wasn't sure it was what I wanted.

Thursday was my day off, and it was such a relief to go back to Haarlem for my catechism lessons. Going home each week only made me realize the contrast between the security of our family and life in the outside world. In some ways, it was disillusioning to me.

I had determined to do my very best as an *au paire*. I wanted to leave often, but I was not a quitter, so I stayed.

One day, however, Willem came to Zandvoort with the news that our oldest aunt, Tante Bep, had died. She had been an invalid in our house for many years and Tante Anna had the full responsibility of nursing her after I left. Now Willem told me that Tante Anna was very tired and should have a long rest.

I told my employer that I must leave at once because I was needed at home. Freedom at last! In my heart I wanted to rejoice that I was going home, but under the circumstances it really didn't seem the proper thing to do.

As Willem took my little bag and we walked away from that house of luxury, I felt no regret. Willem said, "Let's go down to the beach—it's such a glorious day!" And then he began to sing Bach music very loudly.

Somehow I felt it was all right to rejoice inside, but I didn't think it was right to let it show. "Willem, how can you do such a thing? Tante Bep has died and you shouldn't be acting so happy."

"Of course we should be happy, Corrie. A child of God is a citizen of heaven and the attitude of a Christian must be one of praise when someone has died. Our grief for Tante Bep would just be one of selfishness on our part, of grieving for the sake of ourselves."

I knew he was right, and when we arrived at the Beje, it was with our hearts at peace with the knowledge of the glory of Tante Bep's new home in heaven. How good it was to be home! There was a harmony there which was such a contrast with the rich home of my former employer. I realized then why Tante Bep had the type of personality she had. Just a small taste of the life she had led gave me more understanding. We never know until we walk in someone else's shoes.

The Everlasting Arms

There were so many times when the problems of the moment, whether they were small or large, would overwhelm me. I remember a time, not long after Tante Bep's death, when Mother became very ill. I was so worried about her, and in addition I knew there was a large bill which had to be paid within the next few days. People were not interested in buying watches at that time, and Father and I were sitting in the dining room talking things over.

I stared at the familiar red and black tablecloth which had seen happy and sad times. I felt so depressed. Everything was wrong, and there didn't seem to be any good thing which could come out of such a discouraging situation.

"Father, what must we do? Everything is so terrible!"

"Don't forget, Corrie—underneath us are the everlasting arms. We won't fall."

I didn't know that expression and I asked, "Is that in the Bible?"

"It certainly is. Moses spoke those words to the sons of Israel."

"How does that help us right now?" I asked rebelliously.

"Girl, it makes all the difference. Moses tells us in the Book of Deuteronomy that God is a dwelling place. We have the promise of security when His arms are beneath us . . . holding us . . . supporting us . . . strengthening us."

Thirty years later I was lying on a dirty mattress in a concentration camp. It was pitch-dark, and in that restless room Betsie lay so close to me that I could feel her heartbeat. It was irregular and feeble.

I tried to think of something comforting to say to her before we fell asleep, and suddenly I remembered the dining room, the red and black tablecloth, and Father saying in his calm voice, ". . . underneath are the everlasting arms."

"Betsie . . . are you asleep?"

"No, not yet," she said weakly.

"Remember what Father told us: 'God is our dwelling place. Underneath are the everlasting arms.' "

I can't be sure, but I believe she must have smiled in that black barracks.

"Oh, yes, Corrie . . . and they will never leave us."

8

The Best Is Yet to Be

Our concerns reached beyond the borders of Holland. We all wanted to know more about other lands, different languages, and people from contrasting cultures. This interest was stimulated by visitors from many countries, and by reading good books.

During my late teen years a man came to Holland who focused our attention upon foreign missions. His name was Jan Willem Gunning, and he started a movement for "mission study advice." Betsie, Nollie, Willem, and I became involved in groups which he formed. During the summer we went to a conference in Lunteren, a center in the midst of the woods and heather fields. It was so exciting to meet real missionaries from all over the world.

On the first day of meetings, an elderly missionary led the hundreds of people at the conference in group singing, and our own Nollie was chosen to be a soloist.

"Nollie, isn't it thrilling? Imagine—you're going to sing for all those people," I said.

"Oh, Corrie, don't remind me or I won't be able to utter a sound."

It was a new experience for all of us. We listened to the

lectures, and then divided into smaller discussion groups. We chose what we wanted to study, and later used the material in weekly meetings at home. Mission students from a large school led these discussions, and we became great friends with some of them.

Many girls we knew were interested in more than the study groups; the mission students were as new and different as the subjects we were being taught. Unfortunately, there was very little time for dates. In fact, the only time available was two hours before breakfast. I've never been very alert at an early hour, but I learned to accept the challenge of this discipline for the advantages of the friendships.

I slept with a little rope around my toe. When a boy came to meet me when I was still asleep, he pulled the end of the rope which hung outside my window, and I would jerk to attention. Soon we would be walking together over the heather fields of Lunteren, talking about mission activities, and what we wanted to do with our lives. It was innocent enough—but not the part of the conference I would relate to Tante Jans!

One boy, Albert de Neef, had a girl friend who was not very strong. She had gone to her doctor for a physical to find out if she was healthy enough to go to Indonesia, but during the conference she heard that she had been rejected. Those two were very sad, so we invited her to come to the Beje for a visit. She had so much fun with us that she almost forgot her disappointment. However, a year later, during another mission study conference, she was reexamined, and was given approval to go to the mission field.

Because of that little act of hospitality, we became quite popular among the mission students. A new world opened for all four of us when we started a mission study group at home.

We had such good training at those camps. I never dreamed how much this would mean years later, when I became a tramp for the Lord and visited mission fields on five continents.

Beyond the Dikes

My horizons began to stretch. From the camps for missions, we met people from all over the world. Then through the

YMCA in Haarlem, we had further opportunities to know people from other countries and other denominations. The Y was only a building where young men could have meetings, but tourists came from other countries, expecting it to be a hotel. The manager didn't speak English, and many times he brought guests to the Beje, where he knew they would be welcomed. We could exercise our English, broadening our interest in the whole world situation at the same time.

I learned more about Christians who did not have the exact beliefs in some doctrines which we did. As a little girl, I had always thought that the Dutch Reformed Church was the only one which had the right theology. Others could love the Lord, I granted, but they really had a lot to learn!

As my interest in a true ecumenical faith grew, I began to learn about Christians who endured so much for their beliefs. Father once told me of Christians in Russia who were called Stundists. They loved the Lord and were willing to suffer for Jesus. They knew the Bible from cover to cover, and were very strict in their behavior.

Father said, "God has given Russia a great blessing by sending these Christians to that country. They live in the vast area of Siberia in a kind of community life where young and old are trained to glorify the Lord."

It seemed so remote to hear about suffering of Christians. We were free in Holland, and it was difficult for me to imagine Christians in another land undergoing persecution.

More than half a century passed after Father told me about the Stundists. Ellen de Kroon, my secretary and companion, and I went to Russia. We traveled all the way to Tadzhik, far inside Russia near to Siberia, and there we found a lively church, so dedicated to the Lord that it was a light in that dreary land. These people were Stundists, and I remembered Father's story.

A very old woman, stooped with age, a lifetime of extreme hardships written on her face, came to me and said, "Corrie ten Boom, I have prayed daily for you for years."

I was astonished. "How did you know about me?"

"Once I got a Care package from Germany. One of the boxes

was packed with a page from a Christian magazine, and I read about your experiences and the work you do now. God told me to pray faithfully for you."

It never ceases to amaze me the way the Lord creates a bond among believers which reaches across continents, beyond race and color. This spiritual bond is something man has tried to establish with big national or world councils and organized ecumenical movements, but always misses when the Spirit of the Lord is not present.

Sadhu Sundar Singh

A person who influenced my life in my late teens was a man from India. As a boy he was taught to hate Jesus. He knew about God, but the Bible of the Christians was a book which he believed was a gigantic lie. Once he took a Bible and burned it, feeling that with this act, he could publicly declare his scorn of what he believed were the untruths it contained. When missionaries passed him he threw mud on them.

But there was a terrible unrest inside of him; he longed to know God. He told this story about himself:

"Although I had believed that I had done a very good deed by burning the Bible, I felt unhappy. After three days, I couldn't bear it any longer. I rose early in the morning and prayed that if God really existed, He would reveal Himself to me. I wanted to know if there was an existence after death, if there was a heaven. The only way I could know it for sure was to die. So I decided to die.

"I planned to throw myself in front of the train which passed by our house. Then suddenly something unusual happened. The room was filled with a beautiful glow and I saw a man. I thought it might be Buddha, or some other holy man. Then I heard a voice.

" 'How long will you deny Me? I died for you; I have given My life for you.'

"Then I saw His hands—the pierced hands of Jesus Christ. This was the Christ I had imagined as a great man who once lived in Palestine, but who died and disappeared. And yet He now stood before me . . . alive! I saw His face looking at me with love.

"Three days before, I had burned the Bible, and yet He was not angry. I was suddenly changed . . . I saw Him as Christ, the living One, the Savior of the world. I fell on my knees and knew a wonderful peace, which I had never found anywhere before. That was the happiness I had been seeking for such a long time."

When I first heard about Sadhu Singh, the stories seemed to grow, until it was impossible to separate fact from fiction. Then he came to Holland and was asked by some people who were active in mission work to come to a weekend conference at Lunteren. I was so excited about the possibility of hearing him that I went to the conference grounds, although I knew it was booked to capacity.

With a rucksack and a blanket under my arm, I arrived at the entrance to the camp house. A tall student by the name of van Hoogstraten was giving out cards for the rooms. When he came to me I said, "I don't have a reservation, but I can sleep out in the field. I would just like to attend the meetings with the Sadhu."

The student smiled at my determination and said, "Miss ten Boom, there's a room for you. You're welcome here."

This same young student later became a missionary, and died in a Japanese prison camp during World War II. The kindness he showed me was one of his characteristics, and years later he was a blessing to his prison guards. One of his daughters, Connie, later became my first companion for seven years, as I toured the world.

That weekend, as I listened to the Sadhu, I was amazed but disturbed. He told of the visions he had seen—of how he really saw Jesus—at a time when he didn't believe. We had all read about the Apostle Paul's experiences on the road to Damascus, but here was a man who claimed to have had this experience himself.

One boy ventured to ask the question we all wanted to know. "Please, sir, how did Jesus look?"

He put his hand before his eyes and said, "Oh, His eyes, His eyes . . . they are so beautiful." Since then I have longed to see Jesus' eyes.

Nobody moved or spoke. The Sadhu's face was the most Christlike face I've ever seen. It made me happy and sad at the same time.

After the meeting I needed to think, and so I started to walk through the heather by myself, trying to understand all I had heard, questioning my own relationship with God.

As I was walking, I was deep in my own thoughts and almost ran into the Sadhu, who was going for a stroll, too. I worked up my courage to ask him some questions, but soon found he was very easy to talk to. He put me completely at ease.

"Please, Mr. Sadhu, tell me what is wrong with me? I'm a child of God, I have received Jesus as my Savior and I know that my sins are forgiven. I know He is with me for He has said, 'I am with you always 'til the end of the world.' But what's wrong with me? I've never seen a vision or experienced a miracle."

The Sadhu smiled at me. "Sometimes people come to me to see a miracle. When they come now I'll send them to Corrie ten Boom. That I know Jesus is alive and with me is no miracle . . . these eyes have seen Him. But you, who have never seen Him, know His presence. Isn't that a miracle of the Holy Spirit? Look in your Bible at what Jesus said to Thomas in John 20:29: '. . . Blessed are they who did not see, and yet believed.'

"Don't pray for visions; He gives you the assurance of His presence without visions."

It was such a relief to me . . . it seemed as if the Lord had thrown a curtain aside and I could see the light. Yes, it's a tremendous thing that we can know the Lord is with us!

Paul has said, "I know in whom I have believed."

And Peter . . . how beautifully he expressed it:

And though you have never seen Him, yet I know that you love Him. At present you trust Him without being able to see Him, and even now He brings you a joy that words cannot express and which has in it a hint of the glories of

Heaven; and all the time you are receiving the result of your faith in Him—the salvation of your own souls.

1 Peter 1:8, 9 PHILLIPS

Sharing

When I went home after that conference I couldn't wait to tell what I had experienced. It was early in the morning and Tante Anna was still in bed. I woke her up and began to spill out what had happened. I couldn't stop talking.

Betsie and the others heard me and came in, all of us crowding on the bed. I tried to recall everything I had heard and finally, when I paused long enough for anyone to comment, Tante Anna said, "It's just as if you have seen and heard one of the disciples of Jesus."

Father said, "Isn't it wonderful to have such joy here on earth? It's a little foretaste of heaven. Yes, the best is yet to be."

Father often said that after we had shared some particularly rich occurrence.

Years later when Father entered a door of a prison, he said, "Remember, Corrie, the best is yet to be." After ten days Father's spirit stepped out of that prison and into paradise.

The best had arrived.

9

Love and a Sound Mind

It was 1909. The world around us was bursting with change; an American explorer, Robert Peary, had reached the North Pole; the doomed *Lusitania,* one of the largest and most modern ocean liners, was steaming luxuriously across the Atlantic; in Russia the Tsar was beginning a program of persecution against the Jews, while in Palestine a young man, David Ben Gurion, was dreaming of a return of God's chosen people to their ancient land.

The early part of the twentieth century was preparing the way for a surge of science and an upheaval of society. In Holland, however, our attention was upon the birth of a baby princess, Juliana, heiress to the throne.

In man's never-ending quest for man-made peace, the leaders of the world were gathering in The Hague, Holland, to make another attempt to form an international body, where nations might try to solve their disputes.

Nollie, Willem, Betsie, and I were young people intensely involved in our own pursuits, and yet revolving around each other.

Nollie was a naturally gifted teacher; eventually it became her profession. At one time she taught in Haarlem under a

We four in 1910: Nollie, Corrie, Willem, and Betsie.

headmaster who was a very narrow-minded, disagreeable man. It was so painful to see our sweet, fun-loving Nollie become depressed on Sunday evening as she thought of the next day, when she would have to face her school superior again. Her face would get longer and longer, but she knew the children loved her so she continued as a first-grade teacher.

Eventually she went to another school in Amsterdam, and this took her away from home for the first time. She met Flip van Woerden, also a teacher, and they were married. The Lord gave her seven children, and she had a better chance to use her motherly gifts than in the classes at school.

My dear, studious brother, Willem, with his precise beard

and inquiring mind, provided an intellectual stimulus to our conversations and homelife. Although Willem was the natural heir to Father's business, he did not have the inclination toward watchmaking, preferring to study theology instead. Father never pushed his children into work which they didn't want, and consequently Willem did not feel that he was disappointing Father by not following in his footsteps.

We all loved music, but Willem had only one favorite composer—Bach. We learned to sing Bach chorales just as most children learn nursery songs. Nollie sang soprano, Willem, bass, and I, alto. How fortunate we were to have a brother, because Bach with a ladies' trio would have been rather frothy!

Willem did not have any girl friends, so when he told his friends at the university that he had asked Tine to marry him, Karel, his good friend, said, "I never thought you would marry! You never looked at any girl."

When he had been married ten years Willem was called to be a minister for the Jews. He went to Dresden, Germany, and studied in the Delitcheanum. His thesis was written on racial anti-Semitism, a subject which may not have pleased some of his professors. He wrote that the severest pogrom in the entire history of the world could come in Germany. The amazing fact is that this study was presented by Willem in the year 1930, three years before the birth of Hitler's Third Reich.

I admired my brother very much, and sometimes wondered why God hadn't made me an intellectual. Perhaps He could use my simple way of thinking in some way, I thought—but I certainly didn't know how!

When I looked at Betsie, it was usually accompanied by a sigh. Betsie had beautiful curls, my hair was straight. Betsie was neat and lovely, I was put together as an afterthought. How I loved Betsie, who was seven years older than I. She was not able to work hard, because she was weakened by severe anemia, but she managed to accomplish so much.

Betsie could turn a drab room into a place of charm; she could transform a dull happening into a rollicking, amusing story. We were introduced to art at an early age, and Betsie could make an art exhibit a tremendous treat, when she was the guide.

We were so rich in art in Holland, and very conscious of our heritage from the masters of the past. When Betsie took me to the Frans Hals museum in Haarlem, she would point out the beauty of each masterpiece.

"Look, Corrie, at the way Hals paints the faces of his subjects. Aren't they marvelous? And look at their hands—have you ever seen anything more beautiful?"

She would explain to me the exceptional talents of Rembrandt, showing me how he expressed the character of those he painted. Betsie could weave stories through a visit to an art exhibit in such an exciting way that I couldn't wait for the next chapter. It added to the richness of my childhood and the quality of my appreciation for classical art and music.

Betsie didn't promote herself; she remained in the background, always helping and ready with good advice and a sense of humor. Sometimes she assisted Father with his weekly paper, which he wrote for watchmakers, turning an ordinary report on a visit to a factory into an original, humorous story.

The church of our childhood and later years was the *Grote Kerk,* or St. Bavo's, the grand old cathedral which played such an important part in our lives. In the late afternoon there was a service called the "everyday church" which was supposed to last about half an hour. Usually not more than twenty persons attended, but the ministers were obligated to conduct the service for the faithful few. Since it is human nature to forget a job you do not like, sometimes the ministers did not appear.

When I was in my late teens and early twenties, my cousin, Uncle Arnold's son, took his father's job and was usher, or caretaker, of St. Bavo's. He often telephoned me and said, "Corrie, no pastor turned up for the service this afternoon. Please come and help us out."

I remember once when that request came I had a particularly full day at the house and in the shop, and my head was blank of any message I could bring to the small gathering of people. I ran to the kitchen where Betsie was cooking, hoping she would have a suggestion.

"Betsie, what in the world can I tell the people at the cathedral?"

Her answer came without hesitation; it was as if she had prepared it all day. While she told me the sermon, she brushed my coat, fixed my hair, and looked critically at my appearance.

"Keep your coat on, Corrie; your dress isn't too clean. Take Psalm 23 as your subject—'The Lord is my Shepherd.' Sheep can be very stupid, you know. Sometimes they don't see food behind their backs. We need the Lord just as much as sheep need a shepherd."

Betsie told me the whole outline of the sermon while she accompanied me to the door.

"I'll pray for you . . . I'm sure God will bless the message."

I was halfway through the little alley, and turned to see her still standing in the doorway.

"Betsie, I can't think . . . what hymns should I give them to sing?"

"Just ask them for their favorites."

There was a blessing in the cathedral that day, while in the kitchen of our house, Betsie prayed.

She was tidy about her person, her possessions, and her thoughts. I remember years later I passed her cell in the German prison in Holland where we were political prisoners of the Nazi regime. The Red Cross had just sent a food package to the prisoners, and on the little corner shelf stood that food in neat rows. Over a stool was a handkerchief and a bottle with two tulips, a present from the judge with whom Betsie had prayed after the hearing. In those stark surroundings was an atmosphere of cleanliness and order, which was the stamp of Betsie's personality.

Although we had our individual interests, we loved a family project together. Mama and Papa's twenty-fifth anniversary was our chance to plan a real celebration. Nollie had been working as a teacher, and she had to supply the finances for the party. She had saved as much as she could in order to rent the hall of the YMCA. We planned the entertainment, but that was free—except for the personal price of courage I had to pay to perform before all the guests.

Willem came as Johann Sebastian Bach, playing his part with a dignified flourish. He was a musician, and I probably thought it was easy for him. Nollie, who loved to dress up, was Sarah Bernhardt. (Why hadn't I learned those social graces?)

The evening of the party Mother was flushed with excitement; I thought she had never looked more beautiful. Father escorted her to the YMCA as if he were taking the Queen herself to a royal ball. Dozens of friends from the rich to the servant class were at the party; merchants on the street; clients whose clocks Father repaired and wound; people to whom Mother had brought soup and comfort—all swarmed into the hall to bring their love and congratulations to the popular watchmaker and his wife.

When the party was almost over, I finally mustered the nerve to contribute my part to the entertainment. I was introduced with a flourish by Willem and stepped forward in a borrowed Salvation Army uniform. I can't remember whether the uniform fit or I sung on key, but I do know that an edge was taken off my shyness in my first public appearance.

The four of us had pooled our money to buy a silver serviette ring for Father and Mother, which Willem had engraved with a Hebrew inscription. It said: THE LORD IS GOOD. HIS MERCY IS FROM ETERNITY AND HIS FAITHFULNESS FROM GENERATION TO GENERATION.

The Lord was faithful in giving me the strength to sing in front of all those people. I don't think I dreamed when I was seventeen that I would be called to speak before thousands some day. His faithfulness is certainly "from generation to generation."

Ethics, Dogmatics and Bathtubs

In 1910 a Bible school opened in Haarlem. When I saw the program I was so excited. There was so much I wanted to learn. I plunged into this new enterprise, taking seven different subjects at one time. For two years I struggled with ethics, dogmatics, church history, Old Testament, New Testament, story of the Old Testament, and story of the New Testament. Such an undertaking might not be so difficult for a clever student —but that I wasn't.

During this time Mother suffered a slight stroke. Although she became weaker physically, her gentle spirit and positive attitude were an encouragement to all of us.

As my work load at home increased, it became more of a chore to keep up with my studies. Finally the day of judgment arrived—examinations. The first part was practical application; we had to give lessons and answer questions from students. I passed this quite well, and was full of confidence when I appeared before the group of ministers who were to give me the second part of the examination.

The ministers gathered to interrogate me in a room which should have held no terror for me. It was a large conference room opening off a familiar corridor in St. Bavo's. Dot and I had played in that room as children, but when I saw the rather formidable-looking gentlemen sitting on both sides of the massive table my courage began to wither. The fireplace on one side of the room was large enough for me to walk into, but I realized I was no longer a child hiding in the coatroom so the principal wouldn't see me.

The president of the church asked me the first question. "Miss ten Boom, what did you study for ethics?"

"I followed the teaching of Mr. Johnson for two years . . ." I began, but got no further.

St. Bavo's was usually chilly, but the icicles seemed to form on the ceiling. Pastor Williamson, the president, lifted his eyebrows and stared at me. He and Pastor Johnson had been theological students at the same university, and their disagreements were well known among the faculty.

"You studied nothing else?" Pastor Williamson asked disdainfully.

It was tense. I was tense. Suddenly I couldn't remember a thing. Out of seven different subjects I managed to get seven failing grades!

Willem, why didn't I have your brains?

When I returned home with the news of my defeat, Betsie was one of the first to console me. However, I didn't think she gave me the sympathy I deserved because she said, "You must do it again." Something about the way she said it made me repress my objections.

"When you have failed an examination, Corrie, you know your whole life that you have failed; when you do it again, then you know your whole life that you have succeeded and have the diploma."

Eight years later I took the examination again and passed.

The important lesson I learned from my Bible-school experience was that from these organized studies we learn the wisdom of the wise, but not much of the "foolishness of God."

The best learning I had came from teaching. I could serve the church by giving catechism lessons, and preparing people who were to take their confirmation. In the Dutch Reformed Church you do this when you are eighteen years or older. I was also licensed to give Bible lessons in the non-Christian schools. Parents who sent their children to secular schools could elect to have their children take these lessons.

I learned to listen to the Holy Spirit when I prepared for the lessons, and when I talked with the children and young people, my "lessons" were more of a conversation with them than telling what I knew. It was a joy to learn in this way much of the reality of the Gospel. Talking over my experiences with Father and the others was an added training. Besides this important result of that fruitful time, there was the new experience that I received a small amount of money for this and decided to save that special income for a very special project.

When I was growing up there was one luxury I wanted: a flush toilet. Of course we had toilets, one upstairs and one downstairs, but they were the accommodations which necessitated a once-a-month service from the workers in the city sanitation department. As I saved my small salary from the Bible teaching, it was with great anticipation of supplying the Beje with two porcelain pleasures.

Next—a luxury of pure ecstasy—I saved to buy a bathtub! Each room in the house had a bowl to use for washing, but we were very frugal with precious heat during the winter, and there were many mornings when we broke the ice to splash our faces.

When my "bathtub fund" was large enough to buy the splendid fixture, it was a thrilling day at the Beje. The bathtub was equipped with a gas water heater, so that it no longer was necessary to be polar bears to get clean. We had a platform built under the tub so the water would drain out.

Somehow all of those hours struggling over ethics, dogmatics, and all the rest of the subjects which enabled me to teach were worth it to achieve such a magnificent material goal. How I enjoyed that tub!

Patriotism and Prayer

Discussing the truths of the Bible was as natural to our family as talking about sports or current events. It was remarkable how Father found so many contrasting people for his Bible-study groups. It was this willingness to share his time with others which made him so rich with friends.

For three years we had a prayer meeting every Saturday night in Heemstede, a neighboring village. Father, Betsie and I went on the streetcar to the meeting, in hot weather and cold, rain or snow; it was a regular part of our life.

In 1914, war swirled around our little country. Each nation had been trying to increase its own wealth and power for decades, and the threat of a clash was becoming a reality. Only five years had passed since The Hague Peace Conference, and yet all the great powers seemed to believe that threats and force were the tactics to use to get what they wanted. The world was engulfed in a terrifying game of fear.

From the time the Austrian crown prince, Archduke Francis Ferdinand, and his wife were assassinated, one after another of the countries of the world issued declarations of war.

Father continued to pray for the Queen and the government of Holland, as he always had. We were very patriotic and loyal to Queen Wilhelmina and her prime minister, Abraham Kuyper, who was also a prominent theologian.

A division of purpose developed in our weekly prayer group.

"Casper, it's not right to pray for those in government," some of the people said. "The world is evil—Satan is prince of this world and we should only look at the Kingdom of God."

But Father said, "As Christians we are in the world, but not of the world. We must not give over our country to the enemy, because then we would be disobeying 1 Timothy 2 which says, 'First of all, then, I urge that entreaties and prayers, petitions and thanksgivings, be made on behalf of all men, for kings and all who are in authority, in order that we may lead a tranquil and quiet life in all godliness and dignity' " (vs. 1, 2).

As the weeks and months of World War I went on, the pietists became more uncomfortable as Father, Betsie, and I continued to pray for our government. The difference in these basic beliefs drove the group apart. The others began to draw more and more into their spiritual shells, until we could no longer meet together for prayer.

Beyond This World

Father was not quarrelsome about his biblical beliefs, but he stood fast in theological debates, especially with Tante Jans. They used to have some rather lively discussions, which Mother and I didn't enjoy.

Father was a Calvinist and I heard him speak frequently about predestination. I never quite understood what he meant, and one time I asked him, "What is predestination?"

He answered, "The ground on which I build my faith is not in me, but in the faithfulness of God."

That was an answer I enjoyed, and I repeated it many times in the years to follow.

One of the main points of dissension between Father and Tante Jans came over faith and works. In the Book of Philippians it is written: "So then, my beloved, just as you have always obeyed, not as in my presence only, but now much more in my absence, work out your salvation with fear and trembling; for it is God who is at work in you, both to will and to work for His good pleasure" (2:12, 13).

Father talked more about "it is God who is at work in

you . . ." and Tante Jans emphasized "work out your salvation." I believe the fear she had of death may have been the result of never quite believing she had worked hard enough for God.

The Great Journey

One of the great human mysteries I shared with Father was why Tante Jans, a powerful evangelist, a woman with a zeal to teach and write about the Lord Jesus, had such a dread of dying. When the time came when we knew she didn't have much longer on earth, we didn't know how she would react.

Father loved Tante Jans, as we all did, in spite of her crusty manner and argumentative personality.

"Jans," Father patted her wrinkled hand gently, smiling into the no-longer stern face, "are you ready to make the great journey? The doctor has said that it can't be too long before you have to leave us."

Tante Jans's face lit up. "Jesus said, 'I give my sheep everlasting life.' That's good . . . I can't do anything more . . . I'm safe in the hands of the Good Shepherd who gave His life for us. He prepared a mansion in the house of the Father for me."

When the hour of death arrived, God took away her fear.

On the day of her burial the house was full of people who told how she had been used by the Lord to bring them to Him. We told them about the joy she had, and that the fear of death had vanished the moment she knew she had to die. A friend of hers, a nurse, said, "I'm so glad to hear that. I often wonder if in the hour of death the devil will take away my assurance of salvation. I've seen so many Christian people die in agony, attacked by fear, although I knew they were children of God."

Another nurse, who had also come to honor her friend, gave some good advice. "Just tell the Lord that you have this fear . . . then pray that when the hour of death comes for you, Jesus will protect you against any attack of the enemy and that He will give you a clear experience of His presence. He said, 'I am with you always 'til the end of the world.' This prayer will be answered. I've seen many people dying, too. All who prayed this prayer beforehand died in great peace and assurance of Jesus' presence and salvation. I could see it on their faces."

When the second aunt in our family died, it made me think more about time and eternity. We are citizens of heaven—our outlook goes beyond this world. I know the truth of the Bible, when it says that God doesn't give us a spirit of fear, but of power, of love and a sound mind.

Her Silent Love

One morning I was talking to Father about a chance to make some attractive magazine advertisements for our business, when I heard the sound of a crash. I ran into the kitchen and saw Mother slumped by the sink, a large kettle had fallen on the floor. Her left arm hung limply at her side, as she struggled to hold onto the counter.

"Mama, sit down, dear." I helped her to a chair and ran to get Father.

"Hurry . . . something's wrong with Mother."

Father rushed in and put his arms around her. She looked up and whispered in a voice which was barely audible, "Oh, Cas, we've been so happy together."

She thought she was going to die right then. We supported her carefully and guided her to her room. When the doctor had examined her, he comforted us by saying that strokes could be dangerous, but frequently were not so serious. "One of my patients had a stroke and after that went to Switzerland three times. Your mother can live another eight or ten years."

Mother never fully recovered the use of her body after her next stroke, and for the remainder of her earthly life, her speech was limited to one word: "Corrie." With a word, the nod of her head, the opening or closing of her eyes, we saw a display of love which enriched all of us.

We developed a method of communication in which we would try to guess her thoughts, and she would answer with a motion of her head.

It was such a joy to be with her—and my own attitude improved during the three years God allowed Mother to be with us after her most severe stroke. I began to understand what the verse in Romans meant which says, "For I consider that the sufferings of this present time are not worthy to be compared with the glory that is to be revealed to us" (Romans 8:18).

God's glory shone through Mother.

10

Reach Out

Europe was devastated at the end of World War I; there was danger of starvation in war-torn countries, and yet there was also a resurgence of hope in the world. "Make the world safe for democracy" was the slogan of the Allies. The humanitarian compassion of the United States and the victor nations in sending supplies and food prevented millions from going hungry.

In Holland, we were thankful that we were spared from the terrible conflict, but we wanted to reach out with help for those who weren't so fortunate. What could the ten Boom family do?

Germany was a wounded country; many of its children were undernourished and suffering from severe malnutrition. We began to think of ways to provide homes for these children in Holland, building them up with good food and care, before returning them to their own homes. Since Father knew many watchmakers, he discussed with me how we could organize an outreach for children of watchmakers in Germany.

Father was chairman of the international watchmakers, a position he had earned not only because of the respect others in the profession had for him, but also because he was willing to work and keep his promises. After the war, he spent many hours

contacting watchmakers all over Holland to ask them to take a
German child into their homes for a time.

"Why don't you take one yourself, Father?" I asked.

But Father was more realistic. "Just wait, Corrie. Many have
promised to take children but not everyone will be faithful.
We cannot depend on everyone. There will be children for
whom I have no home and we can take them."

When the day came for the children to arrive, Father, Betsie,
and I went to the railway station to see that each child went
with the proper family. What a scene it was. The children stood
on one side, shy, wistful, frightened, and the adults waited
expectantly to find out which ones were to be a part of their
households. One by one names were called, and someone would
step forward to welcome the poor little things. An attempt had
been made to match children with families who had girls and
boys of the same age. I had to struggle to hold back my tears.
Our little Dutch children were so ruddy-cheeked and sturdy
beside the pale, undernourished Germans.

Soon everyone was accounted for—well, almost everyone. I
had been watching one little girl pushing herself into the corner of the waiting room, as if she hoped to become a part of
the woodwork. As each name was called, she tried to make herself less noticeable.

"Father, look at that girl—don't you have anyone left on
your list for her?"

"Let's see . . . no, I don't believe so. We shall take her
home with us."

My mind began to buzz. She could go to Willem's former
room. (He had been married in 1916 to Tine, our doctor's
sister.) I must see about some clothes for her—and perhaps we
still had some dolls left in the attic.

Then we saw another one. A bedraggled little boy was waiting dejectedly for someone to claim him. Father checked his
records, and found out that the mother had become ill in the
house where he was supposed to go. So we took Willy, too.

"Come along, my young friends," Father said. "You need a
good meal and a warm bed."

He reached down and held out his hands to two skinny little children, one about ten and the other a year or two younger. What a sight they made. Four spindly legs raced to keep up with Father's stride as we returned home.

Willy was a street urchin from Berlin. The ten Boom home, modest as it was, must have appeared like a palace to him. When the children sat down to the table and Tante Anna brought them soup, they both picked up their bowls and began to slurp, the excess making rivulets down their dirty chins.

"Corrie, these two must have a bath," Betsie announced, although the need was obvious to anyone who could see or smell.

Willy only spoke German, but the word *bath* must have a universal meaning for little boys, because he looked first at Betsie and then at me. There was sheer panic in his eyes.

Father sensed immediately that Willy thought these two funny ladies were going to subject him to the indignity of washing.

"Come along, sir, I will show you the most magnificent invention of our time!"

I'm sure Willy didn't understand what he was saying, but the tone of his voice and the flourish with which he directed him to the bathroom must have assured him that there was a marvelous treat in store.

After we tucked the children between clean sheets, Betsie, Father, and I went to Mother's room to tell her about the additions to our household. She couldn't understand German, but in the following weeks it was such an inspiration to us to see how she managed to love and help those German children. She could quiet a quarrel with the shake of her head or ease a hurt with outstretched hands.

"Isn't it wonderful," Betsie said, "to have children in the house? And what a blessing it is to have Willy. Father has been so outnumbered by females."

The next challenge soon arrived in the person of Mrs. Treckmann and her two little girls. We had known her through our association with the YMCA, and when she wrote from Germany that she was in desperate need of help, and that her children

1918: Undernourished Germans after the First World War. Mrs. Treckmann with her children, Ruth and Martha.

were suffering from malnutrition, we started to make up more beds at once.

Mrs. Treckmann was more undernourished than her girls, Ruth and Martha. Her face was gaunt and lined with the strain of hardship, which war writes on the bodies and spirits of human beings. *Oh, Lord,* I thought, *don't ever put us through that in Holland. I don't think I would have the personal strength to watch my own family suffer.*

For the weeks their mother was with us in the house, the two little girls were rather difficult to handle. Ruth would throw temper tantrums, which threatened not only the wood paneling on my bedroom door, as she kicked it uncontrollably, but also the peace of our house which was always active—but not with voices of discord. Her mother responded to these outbursts with several solid slaps across her face, which added to Ruth's rebellion.

Through Mrs. Treckmann's actions we came in contact with the German way of discipline. Slapping for the slightest reason produced rather negative results, for Ruth responded with more tantrums.

In some way, without words, Mother taught Mrs. Treckmann that sometimes a beating on the bottom side of the anatomy was healthy, but slapping was not wise.

Mrs. Treckmann finally returned to Germany, but we kept Ruth and Martha, along with Willy and Katy for quite a while. The first time Ruth began her door-kicking, attention-getting tantrums, we ignored her as if she were nothing more than a little fly buzzing around our deaf ears.

No slapping was required. Ruth and Martha became two of the nicest little ladies we ever had.

It was many years later that I received a letter from Ruth. She wrote that she had read some of my books, and remembered the time she was in our house. "What a naughty girl I was, and what love I experienced in your home!" she wrote. "My husband and I pray that we can pass on the love we have received to people who need it. The Lord is our strength. How good to know that."

It was twenty-eight years later and I was in Germany. Another

World War had engulfed the nations, and by this time I knew from horrible firsthand experience what it was to see my family and thousands of others suffer, even more than those in the First World War.

After a meeting in West Berlin I saw a neatly dressed gentleman smiling at me. Something about him jogged my memory. Of course—the little street boy with his slang and naughty eyes!

"Tante Corrie, do you remember me? I'm Willy, who lived with your family many years ago."

There was a new light in his eyes, and I wasn't surprised when he told me what had happened to him.

"I had never heard anyone pray in a house before. I knew that people went into the big cathedrals and said prayers, but when I lived with the ten Booms I heard praying before and after meals, and other times during the day. Many years later I accepted the Lord Jesus as my Savior, but I believe it was because you had planted those seeds of love in that skinny, frightened boy who came out of the slums of Berlin."

The Saddest Day

The children from Germany stayed for a while, building their bodies and healing their spirits, before returning to their homeland. Those were growing years for all of us, but weakening years for Mother. Three years after Mother's severe stroke—times in which her love and patience spoke louder than any sermon—her physical life slipped away from us. Father saw the woman he had loved for so many years, the wife who gave him such strength, leave for her home in heaven.

She had taught us so much. She never pushed Father toward greater success in his business; she sustained him with her encouragement, no matter what trials he had. When money was scarce, she stretched what we had; when we met defeats, she taught us to try again.

Father looked at the woman he loved so much, knowing that she was with Jesus, and that she was free of pain for the first time in many years.

"This is the saddest day of my life," he said. "Thank You, Lord, for giving her to me."

Father's loss was acute, but he did not engulf himself in self-pity. He knew where Mother was and he also knew that the Lord's work had to go on in this world.

11

In and Out of the Watchmaker's Shop

Five . . . six . . . seven . . . eight . . . the chiming clocks in the shop told me it was eight o'clock in the morning. What a wonderful way to start the day . . . with the graceful Frisian clock singing the hour, the sonorous grandfather clock vibrating its bass melody, and a dozen or more pendulums joining the chorus. I hummed a little tune under my breath as I poked the fire under the coffeepot, and brought one slice of white bread, and one of brown bread, out for Father's breakfast. He would descend the narrow staircase in exactly ten minutes. You could regulate your watch by his arrival in the dining room each morning.

This was the day Father wound the clocks in the homes of his wealthy clients. His breakfast must be prompt, for he was as disciplined as the timepieces he treated.

8:10 A.M. "*Goede morgen*, Corrie. You have been busy already, I believe."

He looked at the sacks lined up against the cupboards, and knew that I had been up preparing meals for the day: meat, vegetables, potatoes, and stewed fruit started cooking before breakfast. I would begin the food in boiling water, and then remove it from the stove for a special long-cooking method.

Each pot would be wrapped in sixteen newspaper pages and then enclosed in a towel, sealing in the heat. It was a very effective and efficient way to cook and store food.

After breakfast and prayers, Father would go to our astronomical clock and check his pocket watch. The clock was impressive, taller than Father, with an accuracy which demanded synchronization with the Naval Observatory clock in Amsterdam. Neither cold nor heat affected the astronomical clock.

"Mmm . . . two seconds fast," Father commented. He adjusted his own timepiece precisely in preparation for the work of the day.

His bicycle was dusted, his hat adjusted, and off he went, pedaling intensely down the narrow Haarlem streets, until he reached the homes of his clients in the suburbs of the city. He was an aristocrat and a servant, a gentleman of dignity and a confidante of the most lowly. Class distinction was very strong in Holland, but to him every human being was someone of value.

As he whirred through the streets he waved to many towns-people, endangering the security of his hat in the wind. When he arrived at the first house, breathless, but prompt, he would go to the back door, ring the bell, and greet the servant girl who answered his summons.

"Hannah, how delightful to see your shining face this morning," he would say with a manner as gallant as one approaching royalty.

"Oh, Mister ten Boom, I'm so happy to see you. I've been reading the Book of John—just as you told me—and I have so many questions."

"Good, Hannah. I shall come to the kitchen for coffee at 11 o'clock. Perhaps some of the other servants will want to have a little talk, too."

Father made everyone feel important, and in a home where there were twelve or fourteen servants, a downstairs maid or cook's helper might not have too much feeling of self-worth. Many of them looked forward all week to the arrival of the watchmaker.

His clients were people of means, many of them in the import business or owners of sugarcane plantations in Indonesia. The mistress of one mansion asked him which dancing school he attended, in order to learn how to bow in such a courtly manner.

Dancing school! Imagine such a thing. Father answered, "I never learned to dance, nor did I attend such a school. My father taught me manners."

Formal training had not been a part of Father's background. He left school when he was fourteen years old to become Grandfather's helper in the workshop. He attended night school for a time, but his training was not of a highly intellectual level. He was self-taught, especially from theological books and magazines. Sometimes when Willem explained to his fellow students at the university Father's answer to a problem, he would be asked, "Where did your father study theology?"

Father's horizon was wide, and he talked with even his most outstanding customers with wisdom and insight. He was equally at home in the kitchen and in the beautiful sitting rooms. He understood all these people because of the love in his heart, received through the Holy Spirit. (*See* Romans 5:5.)

Among the customers whose clocks he had to wind, was a distinguished pastor and philosopher, Dominee de Sopper. Father often asked him probing questions. After some months, the Dominee offered to give a course in philosophy in our home; although Father's beliefs didn't agree with this scholar's liberal views, the disputes between them didn't spoil their warm friendship.

For several winters this pastor, who later became professor of philosophy at the University of Leiden, had a weekly study group in our house. There were agnostics, atheists, fundamentalists, and liberals in this group, all with a quest for knowledge and none able to escape Casper ten Boom's direct answers to complex problems. "The Bible says . . ." he would say when the arguments became involved.

Father had nothing against philosophy, for he believed in a philosophy of living based upon the Word of God. However, he would express his differences when others would base their beliefs in such men as Kant and Hegel. Kant, the eighteenth-century German philosopher, had introduced a way of thinking which influenced many in the intellectual community. He did not believe in absolute right and wrong, and questioned whether people could accept things which were beyond their five senses. This would rule out spiritual realities or biblical truths. Hegel pursued the philosophy of relative thinking, which led to the basic political and economic ideas of Karl Marx and Adolf Hitler.

Without formal educational training, Father could debate the most brilliant with the Book he knew so well. He baffled some, converted others, and had the honest respect of all in that unusual study group.

Out of the Frying Pan

When Father returned home after making his clock-winding rounds, I was anxious to hear what had happened.

"What did Mrs. van der Vliet say today? Did you see Pastor de Sopper? What about the cook at the de Boks'—has she been reading the Bible we sent?"

"Oh, Corrie, Corrie," Father laughed, "let's wait until after supper. The thought of the food you prepared this morning sustained me for the last five miles."

My job for many years was to assist Tante Anna in the housekeeping, cooking, cleaning, and nursing. Betsie worked with father in the shop as a bookkeeper, and I pursued the household tasks. I loved housekeeping; I found it challenging and creative. For instance, I tried to beat my own time records in washing and ironing. On Monday my goal was to have the clothes folded and put away by 4 o'clock. If I could make it by 3:30 or 3:45, I would reward myself with an extra fifteen minutes to half an hour of reading. I learned to bake bread, churn butter, and stretch a little to make a lot.

The division of labor at the ten Booms was suddenly changed by a flu epidemic in Holland. All the members of the family became ill. When Betsie was sick, I had to do her work in the shop; this was something I had never done before. I felt as if I had two left hands. It was a different world: meeting people, remembering their particular likes and dislikes, seeing in facts and figures the precarious balance of the family business.

When Betsie was well again, I made a suggestion. "Why don't we exchange jobs for a few months, so I can learn more about shopkeeping? I'm so terribly ignorant of what goes on in the business."

And so we switched. It was 1920; Willem and Tine had their own family, Nollie and Flip had been married a year, and the little German children had returned home. Time for a change.

I loved the work in the shop. The only thing I thought unpractical was that when a customer brought in a broken watch I always had to ask Father, or one of our watchmakers in the workshop, to look at what repairs were needed or broken parts replaced.

"Father, I believe it would be useful if I learned watch repairing—will you teach me the trade of watchmaking?"

Immediately Father agreed. He had a great trust in my abilities.

"Of course I can teach you—and after some time I will send you to Switzerland to work as an apprentice in a factory. I hope you will become a better watchmaker than I am."

Dear Father, he was one of the best watchmakers in all of Holland; he wrote a book about the exact regulation of watches; he edited a weekly watchmaker's paper; he had been a pupil of Howu, one of the world's best clockmakers in his time. How could Father expect me to become better than he?

Tante Anna overheard his remarks and said, "Cas, I must warn you—Corrie will never give her full time to her trade. She always tries to do six things at a time."

Tante Anna was right. She was a woman with singleness of purpose: the comfort of our family. It must have been difficult for her to cope with the many directions of my attention, those ambitions of my heart which ignored the circumstances of our lives. I knew I was the youngest child of a respected businessman who did not have much money, and I was happy and content as such a person. But I believed there was more for me to do.

"Dear Lord," I would pray in the privacy of my little room, "can You use me in some way?"

Blessed Money and Cursed Money

It only took a week for Betsie and me to know that changing jobs was right for both of us. Betsie, with her natural flair for beauty and order, added a new spark to the household. Cupboards were rearranged more efficiently, flowers appeared on the table and in windowboxes; even the meals seemed to have more imagination.

I loved the store and workshop. It had a very special atmosphere, and gradually I began to overcome my shyness and insecurity in meeting people, and enjoyed selling the watches and clocks. There were many ups and downs in the watchmaking business, but Father seemed to have a keen understanding of the economic situation of our times. In his weekly paper, *Christiaan Huygens,* he wrote information and suggestions for others in the business. Since he read all other papers about his trade in German, English, and French, he could adequately fill his paper with important news about trade and business.

However, when it came to making money in his own shop, it wasn't always so simple. He loved his work, but he was not a moneymaker.

Once we were faced with a real financial crisis. A large bill had to be paid, and there simply wasn't enough money. One day a very well-dressed gentleman came into the shop and was looking at some very expensive watches. I stayed in the workshop and prayed, with one ear tuned to the conversation in the front room.

"Mmm . . . this is a fine watch, Mr. ten Boom," the customer said, turning a very costly timepiece over in his hands. "This is just what I've been looking for."

I held my breath as I saw the affluent customer reach into his inner pocket and pull out a thick wad of bills. Praise the Lord—cash! (I saw myself paying the overdue bill, and being relieved of the burden I had been carrying for the past few weeks.)

The blessed customer looked at the watch admiringly and commented, "I had a good watchmaker here in Haarlem . . . his name was van Houten. Perhaps you knew him."

Father nodded his head. He knew almost everyone in Haarlem, especially colleagues.

"Van Houten died and his son took over the business. However, I bought a watch from him which didn't run at all. I sent it back three times, but it was just a lemon. That's why I decided to find another watchmaker."

"Will you show me that watch, please," Father said.

The man took a large watch out of his vest and gave it to Father.

"Now, let me see," Father said, opening the back of the watch. He adjusted something and turned it back to the customer. "There, that was a very little mistake. It will be fine now. Sir, I trust the young watchmaker . . . he is just as good as his father. I think you can encourage him by buying the new watch from him."

"But, ten Boom!" the customer objected.

"This young man has had a difficult time in the trade without his father. If you have a problem with one of his watches, come to me, I'll help you out. Now, I shall give you back your money and you return my watch."

I was horrified. I saw Father take back the watch and give the money to the customer. Then he opened the door for him and bowed deeply in his old-fashioned way.

My heart was where my feet should be as I emerged from the shelter of the workshop.

"Papa! How could you?"

I was so shocked by the enormity of what I had seen and heard, that I reverted to a childhood term.

"Corrie, you know that I brought the Gospel at the burial of Mr. van Houten."

Of course I remembered. It was Father's job to speak at the burials of the watchmakers in Haarlem. He was greatly loved by his colleagues and was also a very good speaker; he always used the occasion to talk about the Lord Jesus.

Father often said that people were touched by eternity when they have seen someone dying. That is an opportunity we should use to tell about Him who is willing to give eternal life.

"Corrie, what do you think that young man would have said when he heard that one of his good customers had gone to Mr. ten Boom? Do you think that the name of the Lord would be honored? There is blessed money and cursed money. Trust the Lord. He owns the cattle on a thousand hills and He will take care of us."

I felt ashamed and knew that Father was right. I wondered if I could ever have that kind of trust. I remembered myself as a child, when I had to go to school for the first time. My fingers were tight on the railing again, not wanting to go the direction God wanted, only to follow my own stubborn path. Could I really trust Him—with an unpaid bill?

"Yes, Father," I answered quietly. Who was I answering? My earthly father or my Father in heaven?

The Trivial Things

As I continued working with Father, we both realized that our characters were formed by our job. Watch repairing is a training in patience. How Father helped me when I had difficulties in the work!

"And who in the whole world should I help with more joy than my own daughter," he often said.

The workshop was opened every morning with prayer and Bible reading. If there were problems, we prayed over them together. Father practiced what Paul advised: ". . . whatever happens, make sure that your everyday life is worthy of the Gospel of Christ" (Philippians 1:27 PHILLIPS).

These simple things kept morale high, but also it was such a joy to experience Jesus' victory. He is a Friend who never leaves us alone.

When my hand was not steady and I had to do a very exact work of putting a frail part of a watch—the balance, for instance—into the movement, I prayed, "Lord Jesus, will You lay Your hand on my hand?" He always did, and our joined hands worked securely. Jesus never fails us for a moment.

I experienced the miracle that the highest potential of God's love and power is available to us in the trivial things of everyday life.

12

All Is Well . . .
Until It Rains

I felt a little strange among the people in that room. Most of
the women at the meeting of the Christian Union of the Lady
Friends of the Young Girl were very dignified, wearing their
beautiful black dresses with high collars and long sleeves. *What
was I doing here?* I thought. I was suddenly very conscious of
my rather low-necked, short-sleeve blouse, which was appropriate for the watchmaker's workshop, but a bit out of place for
a gathering of the *Union des Amies de la Jeune Fille*.

When one lady began to make her speech, I forgot about myself and listened, as she expressed great warmth and love for girls
who needed help and guidance during a time in their lives when
there were possibilities for extremes in good or bad.

In Holland Sunday-school classes ended when one was twelve
or thirteen years old, and YWCA groups were designed for girls
eighteen or older. In those crucial and formative years between
the two age groups there was nothing organized for them in the
Christian world.

Suddenly I felt a finger punching my back and a whispering
voice said, "That's work for you, Corrie ten Boom."

I turned around and looked into the kind eyes of Mrs. Bechtold, a dear old lady who had been a friend of Tante Jans.

"No time," I answered, thinking of the house, the shop, the Bible studies in schools. Oh, dear, I was much, much too busy!

"Talk it over with the Lord," Mrs. Bechtold said.

That was exactly what I did when I went to bed that evening.

Do It

The next day I told Betsie about the meeting and how the Lord had laid it upon my heart to do something about girls in their early teen years. She began to make plans—we had no money, no experience—but we started.

Betsie had taught Sunday school for many years, so it was not difficult for her to get long lists of names of former pupils. She began to talk to her girls about our plans, and in her quiet way she was a tremendous motivator. The first thing we did was to start the Church Walk Club. The youth church on the Bakenessegracht started at 10 o'clock Sunday morning, so we met the girls on a bridge at 8:30, had a long walk to the dunes, played there for a while, and then went to church together.

This was a beginning, but we realized that Sunday was not enough. We talked it over with the children, and decided that on Wednesday evening we would gather at our usual meeting place on the bridge, and walk to Bloemendaal, where some of the wealthy women had said we could use their parks and gardens for games. The grounds of some of those estates were like forest preserves, and it was such a privilege to be able to enjoy them so freely. After each time of fun we would have a talk about the Lord with the girls.

The club grew and grew as girls brought their friends. It began to get around that Tante Kees (my nickname) was "not such a bad sort"—for an adult, that is!

Betsie and I soon realized that we had a serious need for more girls' club leaders. While Betsie gathered names and addresses of former Sunday-school pupils, I found my place for selecting prospects was in the shop. When a young lady bought a watch, or brought one in for repairs, I would find myself looking at her and thinking, "Now I wonder if she's a Christian." As I stood behind the counter and she was sitting in

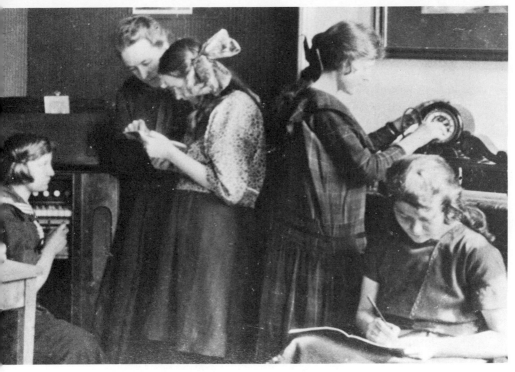

Our first club and clubroom, 1923.

front on a chair, I would start to talk about juvenile delinquency, the need of the Gospel's reaching the whole world, particularly girls twelve to eighteen years of age.

When one of these young ladies seemed interested, I invited her to our leaders' club. Within a short time we had forty leaders. Soon some of them dropped out when they realized their responsibilities, but when the chaff left the wheat remained, and we had an enthusiastic, able group of young women.

Once a week the leaders got together, and everyone had to teach the others the games she knew. I instructed them in giving a Bible message with a short story, and a thought they could use that week. Whenever questions came up, we talked them over together to find the answer. We brought up our problems in our prayers, and didn't depend upon our own resources to work a miracle.

121

These leaders got together a list of former Sunday-school girls and told them about the clubs, where to meet on the bridge, and the name of the park or garden where they would have their game and talk club.

What a beginning we had! It was dynamic—until the rainy month of August started and the entire H.M.C. (*Haarlemse Meisjes Clubs* or Haarlem Girls' Clubs) consisted of dripping-wet leaders who waited in vain on the bridge for the girls who didn't come. We had too many fair-weather girls! We could have given up at that point, but most of us believed if the Lord had directed us into this work, that He wanted us to go on! We were dampened but not drowned!

What we needed was a roof over our heads, and we found a room in a house on the Bakenessegracht. It was close to the Beje, and when supper was over, it only took me a few minutes to run to a meeting. On some Wednesday evenings we had a room jammed with girls, and at other times the place was empty. It was during the "empty" time that our leaders' training club became our leaders' prayer group; we asked the Lord to give us a clubhouse instead of just a clubroom.

Every city has its famous benefactors and in Haarlem the name of *Teyler* was well known. Stories of his wealth, the organizations he had endowed, and his reputation as a promoter of Dutch art were renown. One of the many houses owned by Mr. Teyler had a very large room with many smaller ones around it; from a family viewpoint, it was not a practical home. We asked the regent of the property if we could rent the house —and because we were going to use it for good moral purposes, our offer was quickly accepted. What an answer to prayers!

We had the time of our lives! As we planned together with the girls, they all expressed their different areas of interest. One of the girls, for instance, wanted to learn English. The next week we had an English class started in one of the smaller rooms. The leader of that class was one of our customers in the shop.

The one thing which we couldn't do in the Teyler house was the vigorous physical activity which some girls wanted. So for one evening a week we rented a gymnastic hall in Haarlem with all of the equipment we needed. There we started the athletic clubs for the more adventurous.

God blessed the work. Yes, we made mistakes, but in spite of our blunders, the clubs grew in numbers and in strength.

As a result of my association with those women who had given me that first inspiration, we were made a part of the Christian Union of the Lady Friends of the Young Girl, with international headquarters in Switzerland. Our board of directors consisted of dignified ladies, most of them from the upper strata of society, and very strict in their opinions. However, they had a healthy sense of humor and astonishing flexibility, considering their background.

One of the areas of real challenge for the board was a young spinster with exploding ideas. Her name was Corrie ten Boom. A doctor's wife, Mrs. Burkens, was given the job of "controlling" Corrie, and protecting the larger group from adventures which were considered too dangerous.

Taboo!

Everything went very well with the board, until I came up with an idea which was revolutionary. I wanted to start a club with boys and girls together! Such a thing was unheard-of for a Christian organization; boys belonged in boys' clubs, and girls in girls' clubs, especially during the time of puberty.

Dating had no place in the Christian society; however, a boy and a girl would meet each other in the streets, in secret. After all, I knew a little bit about that—and I will never forget Tante Jans's written tracts after she saw girls flirting in the Barteljorisstraat: *"Jonge Meisjes, Scharrelt Niet!"* ("Young Girls, Don't Flirt!").

The reason we considered having a club for both boys and girls was because the girls themselves were having such fun together, that we began to be concerned that we were raising a spinster society. The leaders' group thought if we started a coed club, that girls would feel free to invite a boyfriend to the club meeting, and wouldn't have to resort to seeing him in secrecy.

I'll never forget the board meeting when I announced that we were starting such a group.

"Corrie, what would some of the parents think?"

"It's never been done before!"

"Corrie, you really surprise us!"

I think I really surprised myself. I pleaded and argued that this was such a good opportunity for real fellowship between the sexes. The only possibility for boys and girls to be with each other was to either meet in the streets, or in the case of bad weather, to meet in the pubs.

I won the battle. However, the board left me with one restriction: for one entire year nobody was allowed to tell about our experiment. At the end of that critical first year, if we didn't have any real problems, we were allowed more publicity. So we started the *Vriendenkring* (The Club of Friends). It may not have been a very clever title, but it was a very popular club. The secrecy of its beginning increased its popularity.

Each evening program of the Friends' Club was unique. My first question was, "Well, what will we do this evening?" Sometimes they discussed rowing on the Spaarne River, but more often the topics centered around politics or the service of the Lord. Somehow young people do not seem to have the same aversion to these topics as their elders.

We had young men of many persuasions; some were communists, while others loved our country and our Queen. Many were faithful church members; others were agnostics or atheists. We had no requirements for joining the clubs, and if they didn't like the short Bible talks, they didn't have to listen.

Once the mixed club decided to climb the tower of the cathedral. I'll never forget how I felt as we climbed the highest steps on the outside of the tower and came into the middle of the pinnacle. I looked down upon the *grote markt*, which blossomed with the wares of the farmers and merchants three times a week, and probably wondered what it would be like to land in a bin of onions!

It was the first and last time I ever gathered courage for such an experiment. Going down was almost a greater nightmare than climbing up, and I may have considered (if I had time) the

De Vriendenkring, a mixed "club of friends" in Haarlem—a real innovation at that time.

reason why the Lord was putting me through such a test of courage.

Boys and girls found each other in the club, and marriage feasts were high points for all of us. Some were married in churches but later told me, "We have forgotten what the minister said, but the things you taught us in the club feast, we understood much better and have remembered them."

Family Leadership

I had an area of concern about the mixed clubs, and that was my own feeling of inadequacy. I knew that the clubhouse needed a director, a substitute father and mother, and I certainly was not equipped for either position. We prayed about it, and out of the *Vriendenkring* came just the right couple.

Wim was a tailor from a family of tailors. His father, brother, and Wim's girlfriend, Fie, worked together in their business. They were such a joy to be around—they loved life and especially liked to celebrate with music. The first days of each week they devoted all of their time to developing their musical interests. The walls of their small tailor shop were covered with musical instruments, such as violins, guitars, and mandolins— even the little nine-year-old daughter joined in the family orchestra.

I had to take one of Father's suits in for alteration one Monday morning, and was invited to sit down and listen to their concert. I was their only audience on that day and after almost an hour, I said, "How long do your concerts last?"

"Oh, we play from eight in the morning until eleven at night most of the time on the first four days of the week."

I wasn't used to this lack of work schedule. "But what about your tailoring business?" I asked.

"Most of the time we start that on Thursday . . . sometimes earlier, sometimes later. That depends on . . . ."

Their mother finished the sentence, ". . . how much we have to eat in the house!"

My business sense was aroused. "Do your customers agree with this long waiting time when they have ordered a suit or a dress?"

"They don't have to wait long," Wim answered. "When we work, all four of us work together. Fie works with us, too." He looked at her with love and pride. "Soon, Tante Corrie, we'll get married and then we are going to live in her room."

I knew Fie's room; it was just an attic in a large apartment house. Not a very pleasant place to begin married life, I thought.

"Well, the room is cheap," Wim said when he saw my concerned face.

"Wim . . . Fie . . . I have an idea. Let's talk about it."

Fie was not only a member of our Friends' Club, she was also a perfect leader of several of the girls' clubs. That Monday morning, in the tailor shop temporarily turned concert hall, we began to dream. If Wim and Fie could live in the big clubhouse and be the directing couple for the H.M.C., not only would some of *their* immediate problems be solved, but also it would establish a permanent chaperone on the premises, which would quiet some of the criticisms we had heard.

Wim and Fie moved in and faithfully directed our clubhouse for many years. They became known as "Uncle Wim and Aunt

Fie," and later their baby daughter became the youngest member of the H.M.C.

All of my spare time was devoted to the clubs. Father and I experienced ups and downs in the watchmaking business, but each evening I always had one or two clubs to attend. When I came home, Betsie and Father were always longing to hear what I had experienced. They were our prayer partners, and we knew that the Beje was home base for prayer support for all the work in the clubs. How we rejoiced together when people who came to the clubs gave their first *yes* to Jesus!

About forty years later I returned to Holland after tramping around the world; in a church one day I met a man who came to me and asked, "Don't you know me? In your *Vriendenkring* I found the Lord. He has never failed me."

Another time a minister saw me in his church and said from the pulpit, "In your club, Corrie, I learned to appreciate the Bible as the living Word of God."

I praised the Lord and chuckled to myself—it was certainly worth the year of being "on trial," and that terrifying climb up the cathedral tower to hear testimonies like that!

13

The Red Cap Club

The quiet years of the early 1920s in our home were punctuated by the sound of Tante Anna's fading alto voice, singing the great old hymns of the church. As the once-vigorous body became weaker, she stayed in bed most of the time, memorizing verse after verse from her worn hymnal. She knew most of the songs slightly, but now learned all the words from the first to the last line. "I've never had time to memorize," she said, "and it's such a joy."

She knew that her time on earth was limited, but she seemed determined to enter heaven with a song on her lips.

When a day in the shop had been particularly difficult, or someone had come to the house burdened with heavy sorrow, it was an encouragement to hear from the little bedroom upstairs the beautiful words:

> He leadeth me, O blessed thought!
> O words with heavenly comfort fraught!
> What e'er I do, where e'er I be,
> Still 'tis God's hand that leadeth me.

After a short, severe illness, God led Tante Anna to her new home in heaven. Father, Betsie, and I sat at the big oval table, once so crowded with all the ten Booms, and talked about the past.

"It's a new life now, Corrie; we must remember the past, but live in anticipation of the future."

Who could be despondent around Father? His positive attitude enlivened the dullest day. I looked at the empty chairs, and began to dream a bit. Mother had always encouraged us in our dreams. I recalled the time Betsie and I had gone to her with an idea we had.

"Mama, when we grow up we want to help children of missionaries. So many of them can't stay with their parents on the mission field, and then they are sent back to Holland to live in those big places where missionary children have their home."

We had recently visited one of those houses, and although the leaders were kind, we felt so sorry for the boys and girls who had to sacrifice because their parents were obeying God by serving in other countries.

I remember how Mother brightened at the thought. She had just left the hospital after a minor operation, and told us about a talk she had with the head nurse.

"My nurse had been a missionary for years and when she heard that I had three daughters she said, 'Mrs. ten Boom, I think you should keep one daughter at home, one should be a deaconess in our hospital, and one you should give to the missions.' "

My eyes grew big at the thought. Which one was I to be?

"What was your answer, Mama?"

"I told the nurse—I would not know if I could give a daughter of mine for the mission field!"

Mother explained the reason for her strong feelings. She continued her story: "My own mother was in Indonesia when she was a little child. Her parents lived there, and both died on the same day. There were three small children left without parents. A black woman took them all to her home, and cared for them for two years before they could find a ship with a captain who was willing to take the three orphans to Holland on his ship, without grown-ups to supervise them. The kind

Negroes who kept my mother and her brother and sister were very good to them, but my mother's childhood was very primitive. If you wish to serve the Lord by educating missionary children, I believe it would be a very worthwhile pursuit, Corrie."

That story and my dream soon leaped into reality. The meanderings of my mind were interrupted by Willem's familiar voice downstairs. "Is anybody home?"

He told us he had something important to tell us, so Betsie, Father, and I gathered in the parlor. Willem began by saying, "As you know, I'm a board member of the Salatiga Dutch East Indies mission."

Oh, dear, was Willem going to go to the mission field?

But that wasn't it at all. His request, I admit, was a strange "coincidence"—coming at that particular time.

"There are three children of missionaries," Willem continued, "who need to have a home on short notice. Their parents must leave for the mission field. They're very clever children, two girls and a boy. Now we can find a home for the boy, but not for the girls. They all need to study, but there isn't much money."

(That was a familiar phrase in our house.)

"This is a faith mission," Willem explained. "When the finances are good the parents can pay; but if there is nothing, then the foster parents must live on faith like the missionaries. I thought perhaps it could be something for you."

"We'll pray about it, Willem," Father replied, pulling on his beard, as he did when he was deep in thought.

Willem knew that he couldn't press Father into a decision before prayer; that was the way decisions were made in our family. However, after supper and prayer I cleared the dishes from the table, as Betsie poured milk into the steaming cups of coffee and Father lit a cigar.

"One girl could sleep in Tante Bep's room," I suggested.

"So, you are already arranging the house," Father chuckled. "If you two agree, I will not refuse. However . . ." and Father paused, perhaps beginning to think of the foolishness of a man in his sixties with two unmarried daughters taking the responsi-

Our first three children. Standing: Hardy, Puck, a visitor, Hans, Aunt Betsie, Frans (an elder brother of the children).

bility of raising young children. ". . . let's not decide too quickly about this."

The next day the mission director visited us.

"Mr. ten Boom . . . ladies," and he bowed gallantly to us, "the board of the missions met last night and thanked the Lord that you are willing to take the two girls."

Father smiled. "Who told you that? Of course, if you have already thanked God, we cannot refuse. When can the children come that we may see them?"

"Tomorrow."

Betsie and I began to rearrange closets, prepare beds, and plan meals before any of us had a chance to question our decision. It was quite clear to us that the Lord meant for us to take the girls, but we hadn't counted on the added surprise in the missionary package.

The next day three children came: Puck, a spirited little girl of eleven, Hans, a twelve-year-old with great intelligence, and Hardy, their fourteen-year-old brother. We loved them from the beginning, responding immediately to their bright minds and willingness to adapt to a new way of life. When they were small, they were educated in Indonesia, where their parents served on the mission field; but when they grew older they were sent back to their home country to boarding school, or to live with families. Naturally, the children preferred families to the schools, so they were eager to please.

We showed Puck and Hans to their rooms, and they began to unpack their few belongings from the little cloth satchels they brought with them. Hardy stayed in the kitchen, looking down at the floor.

"Come along, Hardy, it's time for us to leave," the mission director said.

"Sir," Hardy said softly, looking from Father to the director, "can't I stay in this house with the bearded old man? I had to say good-bye to Mom and Dad; I don't want to say good-bye to Hans and Puck, too."

Father said, "Of course you are staying, young man. You don't think I can run this household full of women all alone, do you?"

And then we were six.

Our quiet, thin little three-story house was suddenly stretching its walls and echoing the activity of three children. The side door swung in and out like the pendulum on one of our clocks, and it was a good sound. Father seemed to increase his productivity with all the chatter and singing going on around him; the entire tempo of our lives picked up.

Betsie and I discussed the division of labor, and it was settled that she would take care of their clothing and food, and I would be responsible for sports and music. I could combine that with my club work. The first thing I did when the children came was to sell my bicycle. I decided to walk a great deal with them, and as long as we didn't have enough money for bicycles for everyone, I intended to train myself and the children to walk where we had to go.

The Alpina watch company had sent us little red caps—the type worn by the Swiss yodelers—and I gave each of the children one of these. The first time we all ventured out on a walk, the conductor of the street car saw us and said, "Well, here comes Corrie and her Red Cap Club."

We bobbed along the streets of Haarlem, and out to the dunes for our hikes, but it wasn't long before there were more red caps added to our little "club."

Along Comes Lessie

Just as we had the children of the watchmakers come to live with us after the First World War, we inherited another girl who had been promised a home in Holland, and then had been rejected. Lessie was a missionary's daughter, who was on a boat ready to sail from Indonesia to Holland, when a telegram came from the uncle she was going to visit, saying that she was not welcome. Her mother was so upset because Lessie needed a time in Holland to begin the training school for teachers, and all the arrangements had been made.

The parents of Hans and Puck were at the ship—bidding Lessie good-bye—when the telegram arrived. "Send her to the Beje," they said. "They always have room, but if they don't, they'll make it."

Consequently we received a letter announcing the arrival of Lessie within two days. There was no time to write our answer; in fact, there was no alternative.

"We have no room for more beds," Betsie said. Her precise nature of housekeeping was straining with the increasingly crowded and cluttered conditions. However, she didn't complain, she moved things, rearranged furniture, and we made do.

"I can sleep in the tower—the place where the suitcases are kept," Hardy said.

A plan was already forming in my mind. "No, we'll put two beds on top of each other in my room." I invented a type of bunk beds with our old bedsteads.

When Lessie arrived, hurt because she had been refused by her one relative, she was welcomed by us with open arms.

Within a short time the Lord chose to send us two more girls. We experienced that with men there are impossible situations and circumstances, but with God all things are possible.

Our Red Cap Club added more caps, and we began to look like a troop of yodelers!

All the girls went into the training school for teachers, and Hardy went to another school, just for boys. Poor Hardy, he was surrounded by girls, and I'm sure he must have felt overwhelmed at times. He began to disappear for several hours at a time, and one day Betsie marched into the kitchen with a frown on her gentle face.

"Do you know what Hardy is doing?"

Oh, dear. I began to imagine all sorts of evil things, none of which seemed to suit Hardy's basic good character.

"He's going to Charlie Chaplin movies!" Betsie announced indignantly.

"To the movies? You don't say!"

None of us had ever been to the movies, but somehow I didn't hold as scandalous a view of this new invention as Betsie did. We didn't forbid Hardy from this pursuit, but we tried to make the activities for the children so attractive that they weren't too interested in such things.

I loved the physical activities with my foster children. When we walked together, we talked together, and it was more valuable than any "lectures" we might give. We had such great fun on our hikes. Once we walked with one of my clubs from Haarlem to Amsterdam, which was a distance of seventeen kilometers (about ten miles). We carried our lunch and sang whenever our spirits began to droop a bit. My foster children were the most enthusiastic.

We had gymnastic lessons, too, although I wasn't a very good pupil myself. My feet never seemed to do what my mind instructed them. We all worked out on the gymnastic bars, with a succession of teachers who taught their individual type of body movements; the German method taught a different style than the French, and both were contrary to the Swedish gym-

Here I am teaching one of those famous gym classes.

nastics. I learned to do a bird's nest on the bars, but I was certainly an awkward bird compared to my club girls.

In the middle of a gymnastic lesson, I would blow my whistle and we would have a Bible lesson which would last from two to five minutes. The lessons were usually in the form of stories that the children could remember—stories which emphasized a Bible truth.

For instance, I told the story about the old monk. "There was an old monk who sang a Christmas song every Christmas Eve for his brothers in the monastery, and for visitors who would come from the village for the special services. His voice was very ugly, but he loved the Lord and sang from his heart. Once the director of the cloister said, 'I'm sorry, Brother Don, we have a new monk who has such a beautiful voice . . . he will sing this Christmas.'

"The man sang so beautifully that everyone was happy.

136

"But that night an angel came to the superior and said, 'Why didn't you have a Christmas Eve song?'

"The superior was very surprised. 'We had a beautiful song, didn't you hear it?'

"The angel shook his head sadly, 'It may have been very inspiring to you, but we didn't hear it in heaven.'

"You see, the old monk with the raspy voice had a personal relationship with the Lord Jesus, but the young monk was singing for his own benefit, not for that of the Lord's."

"That's a good story, Tante Kees," Puck panted while trying to do a backbend and talk at the same time. (She called me by the nickname that all the club girls used.) "Is that in the Bible?"

"No, Puck, but the Bible does say, 'but if any one loves God, he is known by Him' (1 Corinthians 8:3). Do you think that God knew the young monk?"

The girls were in a training school for teachers, and the quick little Bible studies in story form came in very handy for them.

One day they told us about a student in their class who cried a lot. Hans was especially concerned about her, and at supper time, while everyone was around the oval table, she brought up the subject.

"Remember me telling you about Miep, the girl in our class who cries a lot? Well, I talked to her today during recess and found out that she lives with a cousin. Her parents are in Belgium. She can't seem to eat. Anyhow, her cousin told her that she had to finish her meal before she could leave for school, so she's almost always late. She's miserable with her cousin and doesn't want to go back."

"Please, Tante Betsie, Tante Kees, take Miep into our house," Puck said. "She's really so sweet but so unhappy. We can sleep two in a bed."

The next day, Betsie went to visit the cousin and his wife. They were good people, but had very little insight about raising a teenager. They agreed that we should have Miep in our house for a time.

When Miep arrived, Betsie gave her a real welcome. "Look, Miep, no one here has to eat who doesn't want to . . . here is

June 14, 1931. The ten Boom family with foster children.

the bread; whenever you are hungry, you can help yourself and make a sandwich."

Miep soon became a happy, relaxed girl, full of humor and a good, normal appetite.

With seven children in the house now, the Beje was an active, noisy place. In the evenings Father sat in the living room, surrounded by his second family, busily writing his weekly paper. He went about his work oblivious to the din surrounding him, looking up occasionally to smile at one of the children.

The girls were always in a hurry to get to one of their clubs, or to do their studying. They tried to shorten the devotions at night, but Father, called *Opa* by the children, was aware of their methods.

Puck said once, "Opa, let's just read Psalm 117 tonight."

"Well, now, Puck, I just think I'll read Psalm 119."

A visitor commented to Father that he was astonished at all the noise and laughter in our house. Father said, "Our children are such good kids . . . why they never quarrel and are always ready to help each other. They're just angels."

I sighed and went upstairs to talk to Puck, who had been sent to her room for the "angelic" way she had said, "I hate Lessie!"

She was sitting in the corner of her bed, curled up in that defiant position children take when they know they're going to be punished.

"Puck, don't you know that Jesus says hatred is murder in God's eyes. He told us that we must love our enemies," I said.

"Well, I can't love Lessie!"

"In Romans 5:5 Paul says, '. . . the love of God has been poured out within our hearts through the Holy Spirit who was given to us.' If you give room in your heart for the Holy Spirit, He will give you His love, a part of the fruit of the Spirit—and that love never fails."

Puck looked up, a trace of tears in her eyes, "But, Tante Kees, what must I do? Such hateful thoughts come in my heart."

"John says, 'If we confess our sins, he is faithful and just to forgive us our sins, and to cleanse us from all unrighteousness' [1 John 1:9 KJV]. Jesus will cleanse your heart with His blood, and then He will fill you with His love. Shall we go to Him now and tell Him everything?"

Puck relaxed. All the tension in her taut muscles left, and she lowered her head as we prayed together. Puck and Lessie became the greatest of friends. Years later Puck was in a concentration camp in Indonesia, placed there by the Japanese during World War II. The guards were very cruel, and how she needed the Holy Spirit to give her love for her enemies! She was married then and her husband, Fritz, was in a concentration camp in the Philippines. When she was released she only weighed 79 pounds. Fritz survived the years of imprisonment, and was an emaciated 106 pounds when he was freed.

Puck told me after the war, "I always thought if I came out

alive, 'I wonder if my parents in Holland will have the strength to stand the hardships of the war—but I know that Opa and Tante Betsie and Tante Kees will be there.' That gave me a feeling of security. When I was beaten, I thought of you and Opa, and remembered what you had taught me about love for my enemies."

Puck's parents were still alive when she came back after the war. Opa and Tante Betsie were no longer there, but what they had taught Puck lasted. ". . . the righteous shall be in everlasting remembrance" (Psalms 112:6 KJV).

Although Betsie and I never married, we received such love from all of our children and were able to give them so much of our love! However, a house full of teenagers was not uncomplicated. There were many things to talk over with the Lord. Daily. Sometimes there was not much money. When they needed new shoes they had to wait until the finances were available. Cardboard or newspapers temporarily stuffed in the soles were frequent emergency measures.

We shared our sorrows and joys with all of them. When I sold an expensive clock or watch I came to the living room, stood in the door, and made an impressive announcement.

"Ladies—and the two gentlemen present—I wish to inform all of you gathered for this important occasion that Mrs. van der Hoeven has just purchased the gold Alpina, and paid cash for it!"

Cheers. Hurrahs.

"Now I can get my shoes."

"And I my petticoat."

When the situation was serious, we prayed about it, and didn't forget afterward to thank God together. We lived as a real family.

Betsie was wonderful in contacting the parents; she wrote them every week. When one of the girls got a new dress, she took a snapshot, and sent it to the parents together with a piece of material.

Marijke was the only girl who had difficulties in school. She was studying to be a kindergarten teacher and loved children,

Papa with two of his grandchildren. Behind them are Corrie, Hans, Martha Treck-mann, Puck, Betsie, Lessie.

We three with two of our foster children.

but was terrified of examinations. Once she failed, and it was difficult to persuade her to go back the next time.

She adored Opa—as all the children did. The evening before the crucial day of the examination, he was writing his weekly paper and concentrating so intently that it was almost impossible to stir him, except with something very tempting.

He laid down his pen when Puck brought in the tea. She had made cookies, and everyone had to pay attention to such a treat.

"I'm not going to the examination tomorrow," Marijke stated.

"Why not?" Father asked, immediately concerned over one of his children.

"I'll fail again."

142

Father smiled. "Listen, Marijke, you have done your best and possibly you can't do it alone. But Paul said, 'I can do all things through Christ who strengthens me.' Do you think He will give you strength if you trust Him?"

"Paul never had to go to examinations," Hardy remarked with the complete assurance of a teen-age boy who knows all the answers.

"I think his questioning from Felix was a bit tougher than an exam for a kindergarten teacher," Lessie answered, pleased with herself for making this comparison. (We had been studying the Book of Acts.)

"Can you really pray for everything? Even something as little as an examination?" Marijke asked with renewed interest.

Father leaned back in his chair, warming his hands with the steaming tea, relishing the chance to discuss the Scriptures. "Paul says in Philippians 1:27, 'Whatever happens make sure that your everyday life is worthy of the Gospel of Jesus Christ.' When you belong to the Lord, there's not one single thing you have to conquer in your own strength. The hairs of your head are numbered; can anything be more trivial than that?"

"But, Opa," Puck said, "yesterday I didn't learn French because I was busy making the cookies. That was more fun than dull old French. So this morning I prayed that I wouldn't be called on. But God didn't help me. I did get called on and what a mess I made of the French words!"

"I'm not surprised," Father chuckled. "If you didn't learn, you can't expect the Lord to help you."

Hardy added, with a sudden burst of understanding which made me very pleased with him, "I've found out that if I want to pray for something that is wrong, I simply can't."

It was years later that I had to learn another lesson about prayer for something that was not 100 percent right.

It was in 1945, shortly after the war, that I went to Switzerland. I had spoken there in many meetings, but also I visited my former watchmaker friends from whom I had learned my trade many years before. I bought some watches while I was there. In Holland, there was still a severe shortage of imported articles and to buy Swiss watches was rather complicated.

When I put my watches in my suitcase, I smiled because of the methods we had learned in the time of the underground work when we saved Jewish people and hid articles in our luggage. Surely nobody should be able to find my three watches!

Before I went to the train, I prayed the way I always do when I start a trip.

"Lord, protect us against accidents; bless the engineer of the train and give him wisdom; make us a blessing for our fellow travelers, and Lord . . . give us success in smuggling . . . in smug . . . ." (I wanted to say, "In smuggling my watches," but I couldn't.)

The moment I started to pray for it, I knew it was a sin. Smuggling to avoid paying money is the same as stealing. I didn't smuggle my watches and I experienced again that prayer can be a discipline. Praying for something that is wrong is not possible.

As the girls grew older and discovered that boys were more than just a nuisance, it became an increasing challenge to answer their questions. The walks we had together brought a closeness and ease of communication, in spite of our difference in age. Usually we walked on Sunday afternoon, since our week was filled with work and school. I remember when we walked from Haarlem to the dunes near Zandvoort, the sun warm on our faces, and the sand inviting us to sunbathe, we would frequently lie on our backs and talk about . . . well, just the things girls talk about.

"Tante Kees, were you ever engaged to be married?"

"Tante Kees, do you long to have a husband? Do you find it difficult to be single?"

Once they started the girls could ask questions as rapidly as a second hand could move in an accurate timepiece.

"You rascals . . . this is a very important subject to talk about, when you are beginning your lives as young women." I had no sadness or regret, only joy in telling the story of Karel.

"There was a time in my life when I expected to marry a boy

Papa surrounded by foster children. I am right behind him.

who loved me and whom I loved. He was going to be a minister, and was from a big family where several members were clergymen. They had the usual problems that ministers have with finances.

"His mother did not approve of our getting married. She wanted him to marry a rich girl.

"How I struggled with myself at that time! When he introduced me to the wealthy girl he was going to marry, I had the feeling that my heart would never survive such a blow."

"What did you do, Tante Kees?"

"I went to my room and talked it over with the Lord. From what I can remember it was something like this: 'I want, Lord, to belong to You with my body, soul, and mind. I claim Your

victory, Lord Jesus, over that wound which is hurting me. Let
Your victory be demonstrated also in my sex life.'

"I didn't quite analyze what I needed, but the joy is that
with the Lord, it is not necessary to give Him a clear diagnosis
before He knows the cure."

"Did you have an immediate victory?"

"No, there was still a battle—rather severe—but then the
Lord healed me and the pain didn't come back. The Lord gave
and continues to give me a very happy life. I have the love of
all of you—and I love you. My life isn't dull at all. The best
thing is that when Jesus restores such a loss, He gives a fulfillment that is a little bit of heaven—a peace that passes all understanding. From our side it is only necessary to surrender."

After I had told this, Puck said, "Now I understand more
what Opa said yesterday: 'Our times are in His hands.' "

He Brings You Safely Home

It was the middle of May 1940. By that time the children
were all away in their different jobs or married. It was a time of
fear and confusion in our land.

Hitler and Goering had ordered a heavy bombing of Rotterdam—and we were bewildered! The Dutch experienced the first
large-scale airborne attack in the history of warfare.

We were completely unprepared for such an ordeal. On the
morning of May 14, 1940, a German staff officer crossed the
bridge at Rotterdam with a white flag in his hand, and demanded the surrender of the city. He warned that unless it
capitulated, it would be bombed.

While surrender negotiations were actually under way, the
bombers appeared and wiped out the heart of our great city.
Over 800 persons, mostly civilians, were massacred; several
thousand were wounded, and 78,000 homeless. Rotterdam surrendered and then the Dutch armed forces did the same. It was
then our dear Queen Wilhemina and the government members
fled to London.

The German juggernaut was on the move. An army of tanks
larger in size, concentration, and striking ability than any tank

force yet mobilized, started through the Ardennes Forest from the German frontier. We read that these tanks stretched three columns wide, for a hundred miles behind the Rhine, and broke through the French armies headed for the English Channel.

Our Hans was married by then and had two children, and another one on the way. Her husband was a teacher, and they lived in Rotterdam during that terrible bombardment. They fled to a small suburb of Rotterdam, where her third baby was born in a cellar. For a year they lived in that cellar, which formed a bomb shelter.

Hans told me in later years that over and over again she repeated to her children, "Opa taught us, 'When Jesus takes your hand, He keeps you tight. When Jesus keeps you tight, He leads you through your whole life. When Jesus leads you through your life, He brings you safely home.'"

14

Even the Least
of Them . . . .

In addition to the work in the business, the club work, and the care for our children, I continued with the Bible lessons in the schools. One of these classes was for children who had learning difficulties. It was such a joy to know that the Holy Spirit doesn't need a high IQ in a person in order to reveal Himself. Even people of normal or superior intelligence need the Lord to understand the spiritual truths which are only spiritually discerned.

God gave me a great love for the "exceptional children." I remember going to these schools and telling Bible stories, and being rewarded when their faces lit up with sweet and simple happiness.

Sometimes I asked them questions to see if they understood what I told them. Once a feebleminded girl answered a question of mine which might have baffled a person of normal intelligence. I asked, "What is a prophet and what is a priest?"

She said, "They are both messengers between God and man."

I continued, "Then they are the same—a prophet and a priest?"

She thought a while and then answered, "No, a prophet has

his back to God and his face to us—and a priest has his face to
God and his back to us."

I wasn't sure if she had learned that by heart, so I asked her,
"Well, what was I today?"

She said, "You were both—you told us about God and you
were a prophet. Then you prayed. You didn't pray for yourself,
but you prayed for us—then you were a priest."

That was a backward child who answered in that manner!
When you bring the Gospel, it is the Holy Spirit who works.

I tried to teach these children other things with much less
success; one time I started to instruct them about the stars. I
brought some white beans to school and laid them on the table
in the form of constellations. I showed them Orion, and they
looked at the formation of the beans, and all of them knew it
very well. Then one evening I took them outside and said,
"Look, children, there is Orion . . . see it?"

They just shook their heads. "No, Tante Corrie, they are
white beans in the sky."

They never understood what I told them about the stars, but
the truths of the Lord they seemed to understand well.

Whenever you come in contact with feebleminded people,
please tell them that Jesus loves them. They often understand
God's love better than people who have problems because of
their intellectual doubt.

Paul wrote in 1 Corinthians 1:20, 21: "For consider, what
have the philosopher, the writer and the critic of this world to
show for all their wisdom? Has not God made the wisdom of
this world look foolish? For it was after the world in its wisdom
had failed to know God, that He in His Wisdom chose to save
all who would believe by the 'simple-mindedness' of the Gospel
message."

Some Are Forgotten

Father shared my concern, my outreach for the debilitated
and the disturbed. Once he heard from a servant girl about a
woman in a mental hospital who never received a visit from
anyone.

Father, Betsie, and I prayed for this woman and then I made the trip to the hospital. It took me some hours to go there, and when I finally found the woman I discovered that she was clear in her thinking, although a bit mentally disturbed. Also her body was sick, and she couldn't leave her bed.

"May I introduce myself? I'm Corrie ten Boom. I've come to visit you," I said.

She looked up at me with tears of joy in her eyes.

"Did God send you?"

"Yes, I'm sure He did . . . and I'm glad, too, because I would like you to be my friend. Will you?"

"Oh, yes," she said eagerly. "Will you please visit me sometimes? Can you tell me about Jesus?"

I thought for a moment. How much did this woman know? What Bible story could help her? I prayed for inspiration, and then told her about the good shepherd who brought the lost sheep home.

We became real friends, in spite of being such an unequal combination! There I was, a healthy, normal girl, and she was an older woman with a confused mind. I truly believe the Lord brought us together.

Often in the midst of a very busy workday, with the watch repairs stacked on the counter waiting to be done, Father would say to me, "Why don't you visit Alida today? She's come into my mind . . . perhaps she is lonely."

Dear Papa! It meant more work for him, because a visit to this friend of mine took at least four hours of the day.

On one visit we talked at some length about heaven. Two days later the nurse at the hospital called me on the phone. "Alida has died suddenly. Can you give us the address of her relatives?"

I know that tears came to my eyes, but I could thank the Lord that she was now with Him in the beautiful heaven we had so recently talked about. "I'm sorry," I told the nurse, "I don't know anything about Alida's relatives."

"But you were such a close friend," she replied.

"I asked her once if she had sisters and brothers. She told me that years ago they had brought her to the hospital. She had never heard from them again. She didn't know if they were alive, and if so, where they lived."

Father said that evening, "Corrie, I believe that this friendship, and the time you gave that poor woman has shown God's loving kindness for the despised and lost more than any other work you have done. I'm sure it was important in God's eyes."

Just a Boy Named Henk

Henk was a boy who was a member of my Bible class for mentally retarded. He came from a family with eleven children, and it was difficult for his poor tired mother to give him much attention.

It was from this simple little boy that I saw again how the Holy Spirit reveals Himself in such a marvelous way to low-IQ people.

Once I visited Henk at home, and his mother received me with such a thankful manner. "Henk talks so much about the stories you tell in his Bible class. He never remembers anything about any other class, but when he comes from your class he talks to his brothers and sisters about it."

"Is Henk at home?"

"He's in his room upstairs . . . in the corner of the attic. He's there most of the time . . . he's really my easiest boy. We know he'll never become a professor or anything important, but he does work for a salary—he's in a government workshop where he makes clothespins the whole day. Dear Henk, he's so satisfied, but when he's at home the house is so full of noise that he goes to his attic room."

I went upstairs and found Henk on his knees in front of a chair. Before him was an old dirty picture of Jesus on the cross. I stopped at the door to listen, for Henk was singing. His voice was soft and hoarse.

Out of my bondage, sorrow and night, Jesus, I come, Jesus,
    I come;
Into Thy freedom, gladness and light, Jesus, I come to
    Thee.

Out of the depths of ruin untold, into the peace of Thy
    sheltering fold,
Ever Thy glorious face to behold, Jesus, I come to Thee.

I've heard Bach played by Schweitzer, and anthems sung by
gigantic choirs, but at that moment I felt as if I were in a
cathedral with angels surrounding me. I tiptoed back downstairs without disturbing him, praising God again for the love
He brings into the lives of "even the least of them."

Some time later I heard that Henk's mother had gone into
his attic room and found him before the chair, with the picture
of Jesus in his hand. Henk was home with the Lord. When
I heard about his death I wondered if he had been singing,
"Jesus, I come to Thee" at that last moment.

Thirty Years Later

It was after World War II and I was working in East Germany, teaching the Gospel in a huge cathedral. I went into
a counseling area to talk with people individually; there were
many more who needed help waiting outside in another room.
I heard a very noisy discussion, everyone seemed to be talking
too loudly at the same time. Suddenly everything was quiet
and I heard an unusually tender, beautiful voice singing. It was
Henk's hymn in German: "Out of my bondage, sorrow and
night, Jesus, I come."

I opened the door into the room where the inquirers were
waiting and saw a child of about fourteen years of age. Her face
was like an angel, and there was something so moving about her
that many in the room were crying. The girl's mother stood
beside her and held her hand.

When they came into the inquiry room, I found out that the
girl's name was Elsa, and I realized immediately that she was not
a normal child.

"Where did you learn that song, Elsa?" I asked her gently.

"In prison . . . a man taught it to me, and I sang it every
day."

"Why was Elsa in prison?" I asked her mother.

Elsa, a patient at a psychiatric hospital, who sang "Out of my bondage, Jesus, I come" in her cold prison cell.

"My husband is a communist. Elsa is mentally retarded. She loves the Lord Jesus and speaks about Him frequently, but her father is an atheist and a leader in his party, so he had no difficulty putting Elsa in prison. A short while ago we got her out . . . it was so terribly cold in that jail that the guards themselves helped me get Elsa out. They heard and enjoyed her singing, and Elsa was always ready to tell them about her Lord."

My lips quivered as I held Elsa's hands, and I remembered so many things . . . the Bible studies in Holland . . . Henk in his attic room . . . and what Father had often said to me. "Corrie, what you do among these people is of little importance in the eyes of men, but I'm sure in God's eyes it is the most valuable work of all."

154

15

Leaders and Blunders

I loved the activity—the challenge—the excitement of seeing lives changed. The need in the young people was obvious as the clubs multiplied rapidly.

Once a month we had representatives of every club gather to give suggestions and form plans. We had so many interest groups: handcrafts, sewing, piano, harmonium, choir. As a few girls with other talents expressed the need for another group, we would find a leader and begin another club.

I led the music group myself. Music has always been an important part of my life, and it was such a joy for me to work with these girls. Our club had eight members; seven girls worked at a table on harmony and the study of music, while one went to the piano or organ. Consequently, each member had the lengthy chance of five or ten minutes behind the keyboard.

My, what mistakes I made in that club! If I had taught them watch repair, I would have known exactly what I was doing; but the times that I sent a substitute leader my lack of real skill in music was glaringly evident! My substitute was Ann, a lady who had many diplomas from the music academy. When she took my organ and piano club, her trained ears suffered—to put it mildly. Dear Ann, I learned so much from her! She never refused to help me. In her humble and shy way, she lovingly told me of some of the horrible mistakes in instruction I had made. However, she didn't have a critical spirit, and was able to correct me in such a loving manner. This was a gift which set such an example for me.

I loved this music club, but the few-minute message was the important part of the evening for me. These short talks about the Lord weren't deep theological studies, but stories from the Bible and about the lives of other Christians. They were brief on purpose; some of the club members expected this part of the evening, but it wasn't really their cup of tea. They seemed to endure it for the sake of the fun in the clubs.

We had a theme for everything we did: It was "Him in the Midst of the Clubs." This is exactly what we did—put the message in the middle of the meeting. We knew if we gave it at the beginning, some would avoid it by coming late; if we talked of our theme later in the evening, they left early.

However, many seeds fell upon fertile ground, and when club members began to open their hearts and ask questions about Jesus, we decided to start a Catechism Club. In this group, they could learn enough to become a member of the church. Some called it the Confirmation Club.

I especially loved the Heidelberg Catechism (not all of the fifty-two Sundays, but many of them). I translated the old-fashioned and complicated style of expression into everyday language that my girls could understand. It was amazing how they enjoyed it, and how much it became a part of them.

My teaching, however, did not always meet with enthusiasm from the pastors of the churches.

To become a member of the Dutch Reformed Church there was an examination by the pastor in the presence of elders and deacons. The first time I had just a few confirmands, so the pastor invited me to come together with the new members he had trained. It was an interesting experience.

First the pastor asked one of his pupils a simple question. "Who was the first man in the world?"

Silence. Embarrassment.

He hinted by saying, "It starts with *A*."

She replied with a proud smile, "That must be Abram."

The pastor was so humiliated.

My pupils studied the Bible and the catechism very hard. The last few weeks before confirmation, they came several evenings to see me and to repeat what they had learned. One of my confirmands was asked, "Do you know the name of one judge of Israel?"

Without hesitation the boy rattled off the names of Othniel, Ehud, Shamgar, Deborah, and the names of the other judges. The examining board was impressed.

One of my girls was asked to tell the story of one of the judges. She said that Gideon was a very shy and bashful man; and when the angel appeared to him, he told Gideon that because the Lord was with him, he was a mighty man of valor. However, she added, "I would never have chosen him to become a hero. I think he was a sissy. But because the Lord was with him, he was mighty."

Later I heard from the French nanny of the minister's little boy that the pastor came home and declared, "I'll never examine Corrie ten Boom's confirmands and mine together again! I've seldom been so ashamed of the poor results of my teaching."

Later it was more than embarrassment, it became a real collision. I was examining a girl for confirmation and refused to recommend her, because she didn't believe that Jesus had died on the cross. She was very unhappy over my decision and said, "I'm not religious like you, but I'd like to become a member of a church. I think it's dignified and I like that. Besides, my mom is going to give me a new dress for the occasion."

I still refused and she went to the minister, who reversed my decision, and allowed her to become a church member. He said, "I like the idea of a herd. Some are sheep, some are not—but that doesn't matter."

That minister eventually left the pastorate to become a professor of theology at a university.

Leadership Training

As the clubs and the work increased, it became obvious that we must devote more time to leadership training. When we

had our weekly meetings with our leaders, we took turns telling
a story from the Bible while the rest of us criticized. The type
of questions we asked were:

Was the Gospel clear?
How was her first sentence; did it attract attention?
Was there humor?
What help was there for the girls this week?
What importance did the story have for eternity?
Did she describe colors, movements?
Did she draw clear pictures with good illustrations?
Was it an inspiration for action, for faith, for endurance?

Problems were discussed and then there was prayer. All of us
did the work because we loved it; we had so much fun ourselves, but we also understood why it was important. It was a
humble little piece of building the Kingdom of God.

One of the problems we had was that we didn't have enough
able leaders. Another serious one was that it was difficult to
get rid of the wrong ones. The most impossible of all the
leaders was *Kipslang*. The girls gave her that name because she
told the Adam and Eve story by saying that the snake had legs
like a chicken. After that her name became Kipslang (chicken-
snake).

The girls roared with laughter during her story about Adam
and Eve, and she cried with holy indignation over their ridicule.
Weren't girls supposed to be serious when listening to a Bible
story? Kipslang's club was always a sensation. Girls cried often
because of her harsh remarks, and she usually answered by crying also. There was always noise and disorder in her club, and
on one occasion the girls began to throw chairs at each other.
It was quite out of control, but no other club was as popular
because something was always happening there!

It was really remarkable: once we had ten clubs which all
formed as a result of split-ups from Kipslang's club! Dear Kipslang—she was often a headache, but club work certainly prepared her for the future. When I last heard of her, she had

A camp in Holland in July 1934.

been married three years, and had just given birth to her second
set of twins.

Let's Go Camping

During the summer we arranged camps which brought girls
and leaders closer together than all the weekly meetings. Most
of the time we went to the *Bliscap* (an old word for *joy*), which
was a simple log cabin with room for about sixty girls.

The campfires were high spots during our outings. There
we talked about the Lord, sang hymns, and prayed. The girls
were very strict about our campfire time—they were rascals and
"born after the fall," but they always said, "At a campfire you
look into the flames and listen to God."

In the camps and conferences, one of the biggest dangers
was the gossip. We made a camp law and one of the articles
was: "If you must tell something negative about someone else,
first tell ten positive qualities about him."

If a gossiping remark was made during a meal, we simply said, "Pass the salt, if you please."

Our foster children enjoyed the club and camp life with me. All of them were such a great help to us as leaders, and the love between us made it possible for me to depend upon them for so many tasks. It was always such a joy to have them together with the other club girls. Most of them had such good training that later they were able to do club work wherever they were, scattered over the world.

My girls learned some of the basic lessons of life and death at the camps. Toddy and Janny, sisters, had several real aunts in Holland with whom they spent a part of their vacations. Once in a camp with me, they received a phone call from an uncle that their most beloved aunt had died. They had known that her life was in danger for she was a hemophiliac. When she had a wound, the bleeding wouldn't stop, and upon the birth of her first baby she died. She was very young, and the girls were brokenhearted. It was the first time that someone they loved had been taken from them by death.

"Would you like to go to be with your uncle?" I asked.

"Yes, we would. We couldn't enjoy camp anymore—perhaps we can help with the funeral."

"Tomorrow I'll take you to the train. There's no connection tonight," I explained.

I saw their sad young faces and suggested taking a walk over the heather fields. When we were alone, I let them talk and talk about their aunt. I have found this is one of the most important things to do for a person who is grieving—have him talk about the loved one who is gone. Toddy and Janny knew their aunt loved the Lord, and that she had known there was the danger of dying as soon as she had a wound.

I had my little New Testament in the pocket of my uniform and read from Romans 8:28. ". . . all things work together for good to them that love God . . . ."

Also, "These little troubles (which are really so transitory) are winning for us a permanent and glorious reward out of all proportion to our pain" (2 Corinthians 4:17 PHILLIPS).

Toddy and Janny confronted the reality and the glory of

On the way to a Girl Guide camp. From left to right: Alie Terschuuer, a fellow worker; Stien Raaphorst, leader of the backward children; Corrie; Atie van Woerden (Nollie's oldest girl).

death that summer at camp. Some years later Toddy married her uncle, which may seem strange, but he was only nine years older than she. They had several children and a good life together.

Along the River Rhine

One trip (which was unforgettable) was a hiking and camping adventure the club girls had through Germany. All the girls (who could spend the time and money) met each week in our clubhouse to learn the German language. If someone knew a sentence which would be useful when traveling, she would express it to the group, and all the girls would write the sentence in Dutch and in German in their notebooks. Everyone had a little knowledge of the language before we started our trip. I told them the German words and they wrote them down phonetically.

The Rhine River was never so beautiful as it was that summer. I don't believe I've ever enjoyed a trip through a foreign land as much as I did when traveling with girls who had never been outside their country.

Many years later, one of the girls who went on our German trip became seriously ill. In her feverish state she talked about the only foreign country trip she had ever made; it had been the highlight of her life. However, just the recall of that trip didn't help her when she was treading the valley of the shadow of death. There she was not alone, because Jesus was her Savior. She had given her heart to Him in one of the clubs. This was the most important purpose of our club work: to confront each person with Him, who is our only comfort in life and death.

Jesus is the real security in this world, even in the hour we have to leave it.

Blunder Boom

Sometimes I think my middle name is *Blunder*. I made some big mistakes, but I can say that our clubs became a success in spite of me. I loved my girls, and shared many of their joys and difficulties.

As the years passed, and some of our club girls grew older, or others wished to join, some of the teenagers didn't like to belong to a club where "older people" came.

"We must make an age limit for our clubs," some experienced club leaders suggested. "Let's make it twenty-five years."

I protested. I had some fine girls who had already passed that age, and I couldn't stand the idea of being forced to send them away.

"I don't think we should have any limit—let's just consider the ages eight to eighty. Why not?"

One of the Triangle Clubs.

No one challenged me. When I had a fixed opinion, it was almost impossible to dissuade me; consequently, the age limit was never changed.

One blunder (which may have turned into a blessing) was when I chose a campsite rather close to soldiers' quarters. In their free time, the men showed a great interest in the girls. Of course, the girls returned that interest. That's understandable.

One day during that camp we marched through the village at the moment the soldiers came off duty. The boys surrounded us on all sides. An officer who had been one of Tante Jans's protégés years before and had been a daily visitor at the Beje, saw our problem. He took his bicycle and rode beside our group, ordering all the soldiers away. Then he escorted us, until we reached the camp.

That officer was a blessing to me, but I'm not sure all the girls felt the same way. The campfires became quite a problem. When the girls gathered around the fire, we seemed to have soldiers growing out of the trees. It was very difficult to get any

attention from the girls for our talks and singing. I appealed
to the officer for help and he offered, "Every evening I'll send
you two trustworthy sergeants to serve as camp watchers. They'll
report any soldier who comes within a quarter of a mile of your
tents and campfire."

After that two men joined our campfire every evening. They
were never the same men, so the rotation system worked very
well. They told us later that they enjoyed their "girls' club
watch," and there was never a lack of volunteers.

I've sometimes wondered if there was some seed of the Gospel
sown in the hearts of those men. We never know. God can give
a straight blow with a crooked stick. He blesses in spite of our
blunders.

16

Safety Pins
on Uniforms

We used every method we could think of to recruit girls for our clubs. We took lists from school or church; we talked to shopkeepers; we even placed notices in the newspapers. One of our girls, Annie, answered our advertisement when she was only eleven or twelve years old, and remained as a club girl for many years. The advertisement was simple, but it brought results. It read: DO YOU LIKE TO GO ON WALKS? IF YOU WANT TO MEET OTHER GIRLS AND HAVE FUN, COME TO THE TEN BOOM SHOP AT BARTELJORISSTRAAT 19.

The gymnastics club was one of the most popular. I worked out with the girls under the guidance of capable teachers, but I certainly wasn't one of the best pupils. Far from it. My girls were much stronger than I, and how they helped me because of my vain efforts to do some of the exercises.

When the gymnastics club needed a slogan, one of the girls suggested that it should be: WE MAKE STRAIGHT WHAT IS CROOKED. What rascals! They looked at my legs, and then at my face to see if I understood what they meant. We had such great fun together. The teasing made for an easier relationship. We were friends, and when I blew my whistle, they all sat down to listen. Most of them knew very little about the Lord Jesus, and several of them freely admitted that they came for fun and not for spiritual matters.

One time I flopped on the floor after trying some new trick on the bars, and failing miserably. The girls did their best to help Tante Kees accomplish the simple exercises. I spied Greetje sitting cross-legged in the corner and moved wearily toward her. Then I saw that she was crying and I asked her if she wanted to tell me what was wrong.

"My older sister Betty is dying. I have learned so much here about Jesus, but I know she doesn't know anything about Him."

"Tell her," I said.

"But how, Tante Kees; I don't know as much as you do."

"Tell her about the cross where Jesus died to carry the punishment that we earned. Tell Betty that Jesus loves her and has said, 'Come to me all'—and that means Betty, too."

Greetje began to cry harder, but it was her turn to work out on the bars, so she struggled to get up and wiped away the tears. After she was through she came back to me.

"Then what should I do?"

"Ask Betty if she knows that she is a sinner."

"She knows that."

"Tell her that every sinner may come to Jesus. She must ask forgiveness, and then He will make her heart clear. You know what I told you about that today. She must ask Jesus to come into that clear heart. Let her first say: 'Thank You, Jesus, for dying for me.' "

Greetje went back for another workout. The third time we talked I said, "Tell Betty that Jesus has said, 'In my Father's house are many mansions . . . I go to prepare a place for everyone who belongs to me.' When Betty gives her heart to Jesus, she surely belongs to Him."

For several gymnasium evenings, I taught Greetje more about the way to bring Betty to the Lord. After a few weeks, I was invited to come to their home. Greetje greeted me at the door and there was no sign of a distressed little girl. "Tante Kees, come in . . . I want you to see Betty."

Resting on a small bed against the wall was a pale young girl,

A celebration when Princess Juliana was engaged to marry Prince Bernhard in 1937.

smiling at me with the radiance only God can give. "Jesus is in my heart . . . He has forgiven me my sins. Greetje told me all about it."

Some days later that girl died, and again I had to speak at a burial. I praised the Lord that my work in gymnastics with the girls—even though awkward at times—had been used to reach someone before it was too late.

Gradually the clubs began to take on more degree of organization. It was exciting to see that this wasn't the case of formation of an organization first, then imposing upon it the concept of girls' clubs—but of the need coming before the structured format.

Out of the gymnastics club, in particular, came the Girl Guide clubs in Holland. The uniforms, slogan, songs, and mottos were gradually added, but only as there was a necessity for them. We did discover, however, that there was a healthy difference between Boy Scouting and Girl Scouting.

One of our gymnast teachers was a scout leader. I asked him what activities he had with the boys that week, and he showed me some games and taught me some knots. *Oh, well,* I thought, *we can do that.* The next day I taught the knots and played games with my Girl Guides. *This is easy! I'll just ask him each week what he does and copy those activities.*

The next week he told me that he had fastened a strong rope on a tree at the top of a dune, and strung the rope to another tree some distance away. The boys had to climb along that rope from one end to the other. I listened to this idea, but that day it dawned on my stupid mind that Boy Scouting and Girl Scouting were two different things!

The End of the World?

One evening I was meeting with a group of pioneers (the older Girl Guides), when Max, one of our faithful members, ran into the room, late and breathless, her voice high with alarm.

"Tante Kees, there's something wrong with the stars! They're running all over the sky, as if they want to see what is happening on the other side of the horizon."

The girls, excitable creatures that they were, jumped up and ran outside. "Why, those are meteors," I said. "Let's go to the Kenaupark and watch from there . . . we can see better."

We ran to the Kenaupark where our beautiful cherry tree The Bride of Haarlem was, and watched the exciting display of shooting stars.

Pietje said, "I'm scared . . . is it the end of the world?"

"Girls, those are not stars, but meteors, perhaps broken off from other planets. As soon as they enter the earth's atmosphere they are heated, and become luminous like a streak of light."

"Pietje, this isn't a sign of the end of the world, although Jesus has told us that when He comes one of the signs of the time will be terrifying things happening in the heavens. Jesus told us to look for these signs. Peter makes it very practical when he tells us, "Because, my dear friends, you have a hope like this before you, I urge you to make certain that such a Day would find you at peace with God and man, clean and blameless in His sight" (2 Peter 3:14 PHILLIPS).

We returned to the clubhouse, and were seated again in our circle on the floor as the questions began to tumble out. It was an exciting time of sharing, and I was thankful for the shooting stars.

I told about the many signs that Jesus mentioned, and that Luke 21:32 tells us that the generation that will see all these signs shall not pass away, until they are all fulfilled.

Jap was one of the girls who was a deep thinker. "I wonder, Tante Kees, if we are living in the generation when all the signs will be fulfilled, and Christ will return. We should keep our triangle within the circle and not forget it!"

(The triangle represented the three stages of development: social, intellectual, and physical; the circle meant the spiritual development. We emphasized that when the triangle was within the circle, we were in the proper position in our lives as children of God.)

Milly was puzzled; this was only her second time in our club, and she was hearing us speak of spiritual matters which confused her. "What does that mean, about the triangle and the circle," she said. "Are you speaking in a secret language?"

For the first time Mien spoke up. "It means . . . stop trying to work things out for yourself, and ask God to do it. I tried hard, but it didn't help . . . now I have asked Him to manage me."

On Parade

There was one outstanding yearly occasion where my father took a direct part in working with my girls. This was the important Holland holiday on the Queen's birthday.

Our girls on parade with Opa (my father). I am looking out the carriage window.

On August 31, Queen Wilhelmina's birthday, there was a great celebration, with parades and speeches, picnics and fairs. It was an old-fashioned Fourth of July done up in Dutch style. Father, as one of Haarlem's leading citizens, organized the activities of the day, and sat on the platform with the mayor.

Since Father was the chairman of the parade committee, my Girl Guides always had a very prominent place in the lineup. We could display our flag, with the triangle inside the circle, and take that opportunity to explain to anyone who asked what the significance was of our symbol.

On one parade route we marched with an elaborate horse-drawn carriage, resplendent with liveried coachmen. It was so elegant that I couldn't resist poking my head out of the coach window and making a funny face. Father, however, was always dignified, in spite of his prankish daughter.

After Wilhelmina was replaced by her daughter, Juliana, as Queen, the date for the celebration was changed to April 30. Since the following day was May Day, the occasion for the international communist parade, we always arranged for all

170

the banners to be removed so that the Communists couldn't take advantage of our decorations.

Going International

The club work and Girl Guide activities grew each year, until some members of the YMCA in America heard of these efforts and invited me to an international conference in Riga, Latvia. Little Latvia was an independent country then, still able to practice religious freedom. After the communists seized Latvia in 1940, Christian practices were stamped out.

It was in the 1930s when I went to Latvia. On the way to the conference grounds, I was invited to be the guest of two old ladies in their home. Their country had been torn by wars and revolutions, and had changed nationalities several times. During a revolution, the house of the old women had been raided, many of their valuable possessions were destroyed, including their antique wall clock. It had been repaired many times, but never was able to strike the hours. The chain for the weight was hopelessly tangled, and I worked on the clock for quite some time, although I am a repairer of watches, not clocks. It was frustrating, so I talked over the problem with the Lord and He gave me the solution. I can still see the two ladies standing hand in hand, tears of joy on their faces, when they heard their clock strike again. That night, when one of them heard the clock, she awakened the other and whispered, "Father's clock is striking."

How glad I was that I was a watchmaker and could bring some happiness into their lonely lives.

At the conference I learned that I had a lot to learn! I heard about the leadership of Girl Guides in other countries, and felt like a real beginner. The spiritual training, however, was a bit of a disappointment. There was a lot of talk about "character building," until finally I asked, "Don't you think that we miss the purpose, when we tell the girls to be good citizens, but fail to bring them to Jesus Christ?"

To my amazement they changed the program because of that question. The talk about evangelization in the clubs had been planned for the last day, but it was rescheduled for the second day.

When I returned home, we decided to improve our image somewhat and have better uniforms. We made dark-blue uniforms, but if the girls didn't have enough money for that, we said that any navy-blue dress was adequate.

With my own homemade uniform, an orange ribbon substituted for the official Girl Guide's scarf, I went to my second international conference on a mountain near Vienna, Austria. There I met the top leaders of the Girl Guide movement in England, and they were very proper. Once we had an official roll call and I couldn't find my belt. I grabbed a belt from another dress and put that around my waist. We were making a horseshoe march in formation and a Dutch Girl Guide whispered to me in agony when she passed me, "You have two belts —one is hanging on your back."

Suddenly I felt very tacky; I compared my dress with the smart uniforms, perfect to the smallest detail. I began to feel like Alice in Wonderland when she grew into a giant. There I was with two belts, and that glaring orange ribbon fastened to my front with a safety pin.

One of the Girl Guide officers said to me, "I'm glad that I had the chance to meet you and talk on top of this mountain, but if I meet you in such a uniform in London, I will act as if I have never seen you before."

After that experience I realized that this enterprise was too serious to remain amateurish. When I returned to Holland, we asked some prominent and talented women to help us form a national board of directors. We studied handbooks from other areas and held many conferences. Since there were groups of women interested in this work from many different places in Holland, we chose a central meeting place—the railway station in Amsterdam. We could work in the quiet first-class waiting room until the moment our trains left.

But I became concerned about the direction of the Girl Guides. Coming in contact with leaders from other parts of the country, we discovered that "religious instruction" was not acceptable. It was considered propaganda for a religion. We

I, Corrie, leader of the Triangle Girls.

One of our Girl Guide troops.

could have clubs for Christian girls with Christian leaders, but our aim to reach the other girls was made impossible. It seemed that all the club work, Bible studies, conferences, camps, were just preparation for something more. Consequently, a new Christian movement was born.

De Nederlandse Meisjesclubs (Netherlands Girls' Clubs) grew out of the Girl Guide movement, but added the missing dimension. After a few years, the outreach of these clubs burst beyond the borders of Holland and we had six thousand members in the Netherlands East Indies, and eight hundred in the West Indies. Because of our symbol, the name of our club members was *Triangle Girls*.

The first article of our club law was impressed upon many young minds. It was: SEEK YOUR STRENGTH THROUGH PRAYER.

Years later, in a time when camping and parades, conferences and singing, were beautiful memories of peaceful times, I was

174

in a prison cell. Every sound was magnified in the deadly
silence of those cubicles; I realized there was a girl crying next
door. I called to her and said, "Don't cry, be strong . . . we'll
be free soon."

The answer shocked me.

"Tante Kees . . . oh, Tante Kees . . . is that you? I'm
Annie."

I recognized her voice. She was one of my faithful club girls,
who had been arrested after my family and I had been taken
to prison. My heart almost stopped. That poor girl was the last
person I expected to be strong in such a terrible spot. I called
to her through the barriers of the prison walls. "Annie, do you
remember the first article of our club law? 'Seek your strength
through prayer.' "

She stopped crying.

17

Opposition!

Opposition to lives which are yielded to Jesus Christ takes many forms, some dramatic, some subtle. Satan is a clever angel of light, but sometimes he chooses supernatural ways to frighten us into inactivity.

During a time at camp with the girls, I was singing outside of the cabin after lights-out. The song had the words: "Don't be afraid for whatever is coming, your heavenly Father takes care of you."

Suddenly I heard horrible noises around me. It seemed as if among the trees some sort of beings were trying to make me stop. The noises grew and subsided, sending shivers through my body with their weird tones. While I sang, I pleaded with the Lord: "Cover me and protect me with Your blood, Lord Jesus . . . give me the strength to go on singing and speak through me to reach all these girls."

The noises remained and got louder and more ugly, but I didn't stop. I knew that I stood on the front line of battle, but through Jesus, it was victory ground, not defeat or retreat. As soon as I had finished the song, the noises stopped, just as abruptly as they began.

I went to bed and thanked the Lord for His victory. The

next morning I asked the girls if they had heard anything
unusual the previous night. They answered that they had never
heard me sing so beautifully. Nobody heard anything else.

He Never Fails

Many of the girls in the clubs stand out in my memory. Peggy,
for instance, was a member of the gym club who was not able
to pay her dues, although it was only a *dubbeltje* (two cents).
Unfortunately, we found that she stole from the club money,
which was kept in a small box on the windowsill at the clubhouse. I was concerned about Peggy, so I marked a quarter and
left it on the windowsill. When it disappeared, I called Peggy
aside and asked to see her purse. There was the marked quarter.

Peggy had accepted the Lord as her Savior, but she was still
bound to her past and background—a family of so-called down-
and-outers. I told her, "Peggy, a child of God is tempted, but
the difference from those who are not Christians is that God
gives with the temptation a way of escape. He says, 'Confess
your sins, God is faithful and just to forgive . . . .' "

Peggy understood, and right then confessed what she had
done. From that time on, we elected her treasurer of our club
and there was never a cent lost. Peggy really meant business
when she gave her *yes* to Jesus; she trusted Him, and I did, too
—that is why I could trust her. She never failed because Jesus
never failed.

The Only Comfort

Pietje was a hunchback, one of our best-liked club girls.
Although it was a long time ago, I remember her reactions to
the Bible stories. One day we were discussing Exodus 20:5,
where God speaks to the Jewish people about the sins of the
fathers continuing upon the children, grandchildren, and great-
grandchildren. Pietje began to cry, and when I noticed her,
I took her into another room to talk over her troubles.

Pietje's face was very dark as she said, "I am a hunchback
and that was the punishment for my father who has been an
alcoholic."

"But Pietje, did you hear the following verse: 'And showing mercy unto thousands of them that love me, and keep my commandments.' When your father begins to love God he will experience His mercy. You love the Lord, and although you are a hunchback, you are a happy girl, because you experience the mercy and peace in your heart because Jesus lives in you."

When Pietje was in a Bible-study group we read Romans 8:34 and I asked, "Who is our Judge?" They answered, "Jesus!" and I said, "Who is our Advocate?" The answer came from Pietje, "Jesus!" Then she almost shouted, "What a joy! Judge and Advocate is the same! Jesus prays for us, so there is nothing to fear."

One day they sent for me to come quickly because Pietje was in a large ward of a hospital, and they told me she was dying. I knew that she had accepted Jesus as her Savior. As I stood beside her bed I said, "It's such a comfort to know Jesus is our Judge, also our Advocate. How He loves you!"

At that moment I saw the transformation on her face from pain to peace. "Pietje, can you hear me?" I said.

She didn't open her eyes. I couldn't reach her anymore; I prayed with her, laying my hand on her feverish head, and asking the good Shepherd to take His lamb in His arms and carry her straight through the valley of the shadow of death into the house of the Father with many mansions.

When I said, "*Amen*," Pietje opened her eyes for the last time and smiled.

Pietje was still very fresh in my mind and heart when I met the next day with leaders and board members of the YWCA. We talked about club experiences, and then one lady said, "I don't like the method of your clubs in Haarlem. All that preaching you do! I don't think it's right. I believe in Christian surroundings, and bringing girls into a Christian atmosphere— that will attract far more girls than just Bible talks will. I preach by my behavior rather than by what I say."

My answer was, "Romans 10:14 says, '. . . How shall they believe in Him whom they have not heard? and how shall they hear without a preacher?' "

I'm glad that we told Pietje about our Judge and Advocate

Jesus in the time we could still reach her. In the twenty-five years that we did club work, there were at least forty girls who died. Accidents, illnesses, even a murder, were the causes. When I stood at the deathbed of a club girl, I was so thankful that I had redeemed the time when she was still able to listen to the Gospel. Illness, pain, even drugs, during the last part of a person's life may make it impossible for him to hear.

When Pietje died, I was the speaker at her burial. Father had conducted so many burial services for his colleagues that he was able to help me in so many ways. His straightforward testimony was not always appreciated, but when death entered a family, Father was a welcome comforter. When someone dies, people are confronted with eternity and there is the right opportunity to speak about the security of eternal life that only Jesus can give.

Father gave me some practical advice for those sad occasions:

"When your time comes to speak, Corrie, don't hesitate. Many people are moved and nervous, so look for a place where everyone can hear and see you. Step forward without hesitation. Relatives and friends who are left behind must be challenged to repent of their sins and receive Jesus as their Savior."

Yes, opposition comes in strange places and through unusual vehicles: supernatural sounds from the darkness of a forest and even superficial attitudes from the self-righteous.

Doubt

Opposition also came from within. Has there been doubt in my heart? Has there been dryness in my prayer life? Yes, indeed, there has been.

There was a time when I needed a major operation. For some strange reason, I persuaded the surgeon not to give me a general anesthetic, only a local. I didn't realize that this could be such a severe shock to my system. I didn't suffer pain during the operation, but I did have a great deal of tension. For several months afterwards I needed some painful treatments.

In that time my mind and spirit were very low; I couldn't pray; the Bible was uninteresting; church was dull. I remember that my prayers were very short. Most of the time I muttered, "Lord, I can't reach You . . . I can't pray. Lord, I know that You can reach me. Keep me in Your care and help me to be able to pray again soon."

The outward Corrie was the same. I did the club work as I had always done. I worked in the shop, met customers, and carried on all the activities of our busy lives. I don't know if anyone saw what a dark valley I was going through, for I held it inside. I didn't talk over my problems with my family and friends. After all, I thought, they have worries enough. Now I know how stupid that was.

Then a girl, Colly, came to me and asked if she could tell me her troubles. She was a bright girl from a good, hard-working family, and I liked her very much.

"Tante Kees," she said with her head down, "can you help me? For weeks I have been unable to pray. Do you think I'm lost? Do you think I'm no longer a child of God?"

"Colly, you're a child of God and you're not lost. Now sit down and I'll tell you something about myself. I know exactly how you feel, because I'm going through the same problem as you. For several weeks I haven't been able to pray . . . but even though the time has been dark, I know that Jesus is with me and He can reach me. Let's see if there is something in the Bible that can help both of us."

We read Romans 8:26: "The Spirit helps us in our infirmities, for we know not what we should pray, but the Spirit Himself makes intercession for us."

Colly and I both realized that the Holy Spirit helps us with our daily problems and in our prayer problems. When we are totally inadequate, the Spirit is interceding with God the Father for us. The burden of guilt was taken from Colly and me, and together we thanked the Lord that He had forgiven us and restored our communication with Him.

Haarlemsche Meisjesclubs

The H.M.C. (Haarlem Girls' Clubs) had a performance once each year in the concert hall, when each club demonstrated some of its skills and abilities. We opened the program with all of the 250 to 300 girls marching onto the platform. They sang a song, and I gave a five-minute talk to the people in the auditorium.

The mixed club (which had passed the "year's trial" without any serious mishaps) provided the orchestra for the musical part of our entertainment. The first time this group had to play before all of those friends and relatives (about a thousand of them), they were frozen with stage fright. I walked over and picked up a violin and acted as if I were a real virtuoso, but making sure that no one in the audience saw that the bow was turned upside down and not touching the strings. As I "played" the violin, the boys gained confidence and began to perform. The ones who were playing wind instruments probably had trouble stifling their laughter in order to make music.

Tears and laughter, opposition and support—the clubs taught those young men and women preparation for life.

When the war started, we had to close the H.M.C. clubs. I will never forget the evening we were together for the last time. We saluted our flag, with tears running down our cheeks, and then folded it carefully, and hid it in a secret closet of the clubhouse.

As we sang the national hymn for the last time together, the girls had a very difficult time. "Girls, we mustn't cry," I said. "We had great fun in the clubs, but it wasn't just for a good time that we have come together. We have learned the important facts of what makes us strong, even in times of disaster. The Lord Jesus gives us security even in the insecurity of wartime."

I looked at those girls and wondered—would they draw on the Lord's strength in the days and years to come? What was in store for them in this world of ours which is filled with hatred and cruelty?

I was so grateful that the time in our clubs had not been wasted in just building "good citizens," but that we had the opportunity to learn the vital message of Jesus' victory, which would give strength for the suffering which awaited many of us.

18

". . . He Took My Hand"

War. It was early in the morning when we heard the bombs. We knew the sound of the explosions were coming from Schiphol, the airport near Haarlem. I ran to Betsie's room and found her sitting up in bed, pale and shaking. We put our arms around each other and trembled with each blast; the wavering red glow was so eerie in the darkness of our once-peaceful skies.

We were afraid, but had learned from childhood how to cast our burdens on the Lord. We prayed like frightened children, running to their father for help and protection.

"Lord, make us strong . . . give us strength to help others."

"Lord, take away our fear. Give us trust."

It was a crisis of fear in both of us, but Jesus gave us the victory over it. We were never so frightened as we were during that night, not even when war and occupation destroyed our whole family life, and everything we had known for more than a half a century. Was that night the Lord's way of inoculating us in preparation for the future?

In the five days of war that followed, many people came to the house; Father was a pillar of strength for all of them; he prayed with everyone who asked. Sometimes the shock of what was happening would engulf me, and while Father was bringing trust and peace to those in turmoil, I would go to the piano and play Bach. No other music gave me so much rest.

The darkest time during those five days was when our royal family left, our Queen Wilhelmina for England and Crown Princess Juliana for Canada. We knew then that our case was hopeless.

There were not many times that I cried, but when I heard about the royal family leaving the country, I was heartbroken and wept. For the Dutch people the Queen was our security— we loved her.

Then Holland surrendered. I walked in the street with Father, and everyone was talking to everyone else. In that moment there was a oneness which I had never seen before. We were together in the great suffering, humiliation, and defeat of our nation. Although my heart was aching with misery, there was encouragement that people could be so united.

In the millennium we will be like that: The whole world will be covered with the knowledge of God like the waters cover the bottom of the sea. The oneness will not be in misery, but in our communion with the Lord.

The German army marched through the Barteljorisstraat: tanks, cannons, cavalry, and hundreds and hundreds of soldiers. The narrow little street where Dot and I had played games—the alley where I had seen the drunks when I was only five, and prayed for "all the people in the Smedestraat"—the path we had taken on Sunday to St. Bavo's—all were filled with soldiers.

As the conquerors swept in, I noticed some of them were red-faced, shame written in their expressions. After the war a German told me, "With every step I took in Holland, I felt ashamed. I knew I was occupying a neutral nation."

Churches were packed in those days; the Psalms, which were written in times of great suffering, gained a new value. Ministers who had never preached about the Second Coming of Christ now chose their texts from the many places in the Bible on that subject.

In the beginning, we saw little change in our daily life, but gradually the enemy began to impose restrictions. At first the curfew was ten o'clock, which was not difficult for us, but later it was moved back to eight, then six. No one could leave his house; there was absolute blackout, and every window was covered with black paper as soon as the sun was down.

Telephones were cut off; food was rationed; and often after standing in long lines with our ration cards, we would find that the stores were empty.

One beautiful Sunday afternoon Betsie, Father, and I were walking through our park, south of Haarlem, when the Gestapo descended and took all of the young fathers around us, who were out walking with their families, leaving distraught wives and crying children behind.

All Dutch people have bicycles, and sometimes the Gestapo set up a bicycle blockade. Everyone who rode by was summoned to give up his vehicle. If you were fortunate enough to keep your bicycle, you learned to ride without tires, because they were confiscated and taken to Germany.

We were not even safe in church. Once during a service in the cathedral, the Germans guarded the doors so that nobody could move. Then they opened one door and ordered every man from eighteen to forty to come out. They were sent that same day to Germany—many of these men were never seen again.

The occupation—the underground movement to save Jews—the concentration camps—all of these are documented in *A Prisoner and Yet* . . . , and in my book and the movie, *The Hiding Place*.

For more than thirty years since World War II, I have been a tramp for the Lord in more than sixty countries on all the continents of this troubled world. Many people have asked me about my childhood, youth, and the years before *The Hiding Place*. A person doesn't spring into existence at the age of fifty; there are years of preparation, years of experience, which God uses in ways we may never know until we meet Him face to face.

However, from the perspective of over eighty years of living, I have had the marvelous opportunity to discover the sweetness of some of the fruit of His labor. Just recently I have heard from by letter or met in person some of my club "girls." (They are still girls to me!) It has been like a letter from the Lord.

Aukje

One of our faithful club girls was quiet Aukje. She was a peacemaker who could say a few words, but make them count. When other girls were unruly and stubborn, I remember Aukje saying, "Don't be so stupid. Why did we come to the club in the first place? Most of us want to have fun and learn something, so if you don't like it then leave and let the rest of us enjoy the club."

To the point—but said with such kindness that most of the time the problems were overcome. When she was about seventeen, Aukje became a club leader herself and led a group of girls who learned handcrafts. She was so quiet and gentle that we didn't expect exciting results from her, but her love for the Lord was very clear.

When the ten Boom family was arrested Aukje came to our house, not knowing that it was a Gestapo trap. She was taken to the police station, and spent a week with our oldest Jewish underground girl, Mary, who had been in the hiding place, but was later arrested in the street.

Aukje talked to Mary about the Lord Jesus. She told her that Jesus had died on the cross for the sins of the whole world, and that He had said, "Come to me, all who are heavy laden, I will give you rest."

Mary said, "I heard Grandpa ten Boom pray so often when I was in the Beje. He always said to me, 'Mary, you are a Jew; you will not change that if you invite the Lord Jesus into your heart. On His divine side He was the Son of God, but on his human side He was a Jew.'"

Mary received Jesus as her Savior in that cell. Our quiet Aukje had a boldness for the Lord. She told me later that the moment Mary said her *yes* to Jesus in her prayer of accepting Him, the guards came into the cell and took her away. We heard later that she was sent to Poland where she died.

I heard nothing from Aukje for many years. What a surprise it was for me when she came to my room in Haarlem thirty years later. She told me that she was working in a small village where there was no minister; she preaches every Sunday for the little congregation. She said, "What I learned in your clubs I still use when I teach the children and have my Bible-study groups."

Poes

Poes was an outgoing little rascal; wherever she was in a club there was laughing and fun. At camp she was the happy note, even when it was raining and attitudes were down. When there were weaker girls who needed help in hikes or gymnastics, Poes was always ready to help.

I remember one time she was walking behind me, and was quite outspoken in her ideas about my legs. She said, "If I had such legs, I should decide to march beside them." She married an older boy and moved to South Africa. I met them there once after the war, but only briefly. He called himself an atheist, but did not object when Poes and I shared with him our love for the Lord Jesus. I promised to pray for him, but in later correspondence Poes never mentioned that he was interested in spiritual affairs.

Then a strange thing happened—one of those "coincidents," which are such a marvelous part of God's plan. Poes and her husband were walking in the streets of Johannesburg, when a boy asked them to buy a raffle ticket to raise money for a house for a boys' club. Poes said, "Sure, I enjoyed clubs when I was a girl—I hope you have a lot of fun in your new cabin."

Later she found out that they had the ticket which won the first prize in the raffle—it was a round-trip plane ride for two to the Netherlands! And so it happened that one day they stood in my room in Holland. What memories we shared! Poes told me she had become a member of a church, and Henk, her husband, listened with amusement as we talked about the clubs. He declared very strongly that he didn't believe in God. I knew I had only one chance to bring him the Gospel, so I said, "Henk, I'll probably only have this one time to talk with you. There are two ways to live: you can go your way or God's way; you can accept Jesus Christ as your Savior, and He will make you a child of God. Then you can bring Him all your sins, and ask and get forgiveness. He makes sure you're a child of God, and He will put your name in the book of life."

After I prayed with them, Henk said, "I believe it's time that I gave my heart to Jesus. I've seen much of Him in the life of Poes, and He must be a reality. I know I'm a sinner and you said that Jesus accepts sinners. So I'll tell Him all that I've done and I have been, and believe that He will make me a child of God."

They returned to South Africa and Henk became a member of a lively church. Some months ago Henk died, but he said, "Tell Tante Kees that God has used her to bring me to the Lord."

God began working years before in a mischievous little girl, Poes, in a gymnastics club in a little Dutch town.

The Golden Tea Party

What would they be like? Would the years have changed them? What joys and sorrows, trials and triumphs would they have seen in the decades since we had last met?

I was as excited as that younger Corrie had been, when she introduced her club girls at the yearly performance in the Haarlem concert hall. Now in my eighties, I had returned to Holland for a visit, and had invited those women who had been in clubs in years past—and were still in the vicinity of Haarlem —to my house for tea.

No uniform with two belts and a safety pin this time! I wore my best red and white silk summer dress, and made sure that not one thing would mar my appearance.

They arrived at the front door at the same time. Some came on their big old-fashioned bicycles, some drove little cars, and others walked from the bus stop. There was no need for protocol, for they began to laugh and talk all at once.

What an afternoon we had! Each girl told a little of her story, ending on the same theme, which added so much joy to my heart.

Ariapja, whose nickname was *Jap,* bubbled with her enthusiasm about the club work. She told how she first became a part of our group and her mother had said, "You may not have a uniform!"

So she went to her first camp feeling a bit ashamed, because she wasn't dressed like the rest of the girls. It was the most important issue in her life then. Hank, who had also come for tea that afternoon, was the one who gave Jap her uniform; that unselfish act was remembered by Jap all her life. When she went home she asked her mother if she could be a Girl Guide. Her mother told her that it was all right, if she didn't wear the uniform on Sunday.

Girl Guiding became Jap's life, and she told us that sunny afternoon in my living room in Holland that much she learned as a young girl in the clubs had prepared her for her total life experiences.

Stien had gone to one of my clubs when she was sixteen to learn the catechism. I had been her teacher, and after she was received into the Dutch Reformed church I said, "Now, Stien, you must lead a club."

After Stien had been one of our club leaders she took the initiative, and began a club for feebleminded children. She told me later, "You had taught me, Tante Kees, to love those less fortunate, and I truly did love those children." For Stien going to the clubs was the best part of her young life. Her home was never open to others, and she spent many evenings at the Beje. Fortunately, she had stayed at home on that fateful day in February 1944, when the Gestapo paid us an unwelcome visit.

Annie, who had answered a newspaper advertisement to join a club, said that she came for fun, and not for all those "spiritual things." And she did have fun! She joined the singing club, the English club, and the gymnastics club, and when she told about the latter, she reminded all of us about the club slogan. (I knew someone would bring that up—the rascals!) The gymnastics club slogan—WE MAKE STRAIGHT WHAT IS CROOKED—was not very good— too long to put on a program. (I had to pretend not to notice the laughter every time it was mentioned.)

Annie told how she fell in love with the gym teacher. However, when his girl friend came Annie became very jealous, and out of spite sewed his pants together and put water in his shoes.

(Tea cups almost fell off laps when this story was recounted.)

As a punishment, I told Annie that she would not be allowed to go to the club for three weeks. She reminded me, however, that she returned in one week, proving that Tante Kees's discipline was sometimes a little lax.

When Annie was seventeen, she was at the camp at Bliscap, feeling very low. She had just split up with her current boyfriend, and thought it was the end of the world. She remembered that we were sitting outside, looking at the stars, and I had told her, "When you're in need and don't know the answer, tell the Lord about it. He has your past, present, and future in His hands." It was then that Annie accepted Jesus Christ as her Savior; she said that every time she was in need in years to come she remembered that moment.

"I know the Lord is willing to take your life in His hands when you're small," Annie said.

Nellie was born in Germany, and didn't come to Holland until she was fourteen years old. She came into the clubs when she was eighteen, not as a believer in Jesus Christ, but found Him during one of the camps. When Nellie remembered the outstanding experiences of her club time, she talked about the campfires—the time of deep discussions together. She thought a while when we asked what club work had prepared her for. Then she remembered one of the articles in the club law, which was to "give help" to others. She said that even today people know there is help in her home. "Let's go over to Nell's—she always has the soup on . . . ."

As the girls began to share more and more of their memories and their later life experiences, one story after another spilled out. Reina told how she loved the circle and the club song. It was difficult for Ellen de Kroon, my secretary, and Carole Carlson to contain themselves as we all stood up and joined hands to repeat our motto, and sing our song after almost forty years of separation! The voices may have changed a bit, but the fervor was still there!

Reina said she had come from a Christian family, but the club work had inspired in her the personal desire to bring the Gospel to other girls.

"Did you know," she said, looking around the room, "that the last time the Girl Guides wore their uniforms was at my wedding?"

Hank was in at the start of the clubs, and remembered the first camp experience she had. One of the girls had trouble with sleepwalking, and she told how Tante Kees had been so concerned about her, and had walked her gently back to bed. However, it was also discovered that the so-called sleepwalker had a sweet tooth, for the following morning the chocolate bars, which had been left out for campfire treats, had been strangely consumed by someone in her sleep.

Julie had been rather quiet, but finally began to bring the conversation back to the present. "I want so much to give our young people some of the love, the experiences, the strength in knowing the Lord, that we learned in your clubs, Tante Kees. Our children have so much—and yet they're so poor. They're so free today—much more so than we were—and yet they face many more dangers from the world."

It became very still in the room. Everyone had her own thoughts about children, grandchildren—our youth, who face the "wars and rumors of wars" that exist in a world racing toward self-destruction.

I looked through my small living room into the dining room, where Papa's portrait hangs. I could see him at the oval table, head bowed, praying: "Lord, bless the Queen; we thank You for this beautiful Lord's Day, and for the promise of Your soon coming. Thank You for this food, and for this family. In the Name of Jesus Christ, *Amen.*"

How grateful I am to have lived in my Father's house! Yes, Lord, I thank You for this family. I looked at my friends, gathered for an afternoon of tea and memories, and thanked the Lord for the family of believers all over this globe. How the love of God stretched in and out of the watchmaker's shop to all parts of the world—to mansions in California and hospitals in Kenya, from queens to prison guards.

As the "golden tea party" ended, and the club girls left, we broke some of our Dutch restraint and hugged each other. Many of them had suffered much through the years, and yet they had remained strong in the Lord. I realized that all we do through our own strength has to be cleansed, but what we do through the Lord has value for time and eternity.

This is no time to look back. What challenges we have today! I remember what Father often said:

> *When Jesus takes your hand He keeps you tight. When Jesus keeps you tight He leads you through life. When Jesus leads you through life He brings you safely home.*